M000224101

ALL RIGHT NOW

Foruli Codex

Published by Foruli Codex

FIRST EDITION

ISBN 978-1-905792-62-7

Cover copyright © Foruli Ltd 2015
Volume copyright © Foruli Ltd 2015
Text copyright © Andy Fraser and Mark Hughes 2015

The right of Andy Fraser and Mark Hughes to be identified as the author of this work has been asserted by them in accordance with the Copyright, Designs and Patents Act 1988.

All rights reserved. No part of this publication may be reproduced, stored in or introduced into a retrieval system, or transmitted, in any form or by any means (electronic, mechanical, photocopying, recording or otherwise), without the prior written permission of the publisher. This book is sold subject to the condition that it shall not, by way of trade or otherwise, be lent, re-sold, hired out, or otherwise circulated without the publisher's prior written consent in any form of binding or cover other than that in which it is published and without a similar condition including this condition being imposed on the subsequent purchaser.

A CIP catalogue record for this book is available from the British Library

Edited by Karl French

Cover & design by Andy Vella at Velladesign (www.velladesign.com)

Printed by Lightning Source

Foruli Codex is an imprint of Foruli Ltd, London

www.forulicodex.com

ANDY FRASER
with MARK HUGHES

ALL RIGHT NOW:
LIFE, DEATH, AND LIFE AGAIN

Foruli Codex

CONTENTS

CONTENTS

I used to be very ill. Back in the early 90s I had viral load of 3.4 million and was down to one T-cell. Any doctor will tell you they are insane numbers. There are pictures of me from that time where I look like I'm about to become the next AIDS death. There were even rumours on the internet that I *had* died. But now I'm healthy. It's all right now.

There was a time – a long time – when I struggled with my sexuality. In Free, I'd been part of a very macho scene and had not even allowed the question into my head – of course I was hetero; I was having sex with a different girl each night. Then after Free I got married and we had two beautiful girls. But something was nagging away and it was only after Ri and I split that I even started coming to terms with the fact that I might be gay. I couldn't be; I fought the very idea. But you can't – and it took me many desperate years to realise this, years when I even meticulously planned my suicide. But today I'm completely at ease with it – I'm a gay man. It's all right now.

All Right Now. I was seventeen when I created that song, with a little bit of help from Paul Rodgers. It was a throwaway song, took just a few minutes. The chorus came into my head as a sort of soothing mantra after we'd walked off stage to the sound of our own footsteps and everyone was down. In the dressing room afterwards I just wanted to pull us all out of it, just started this little chant – 'All Right Now' – like you might calm a child that's upset. It grew from a little sound in the back of my head to something bigger, more insistent, louder and in no time at all I was up, grooving. Some time later Paul put a few teenage fantasy lyrics to it – and there it was, the song that set the four of us up for life.

How many seventeen-year-olds have stood on stage at Madison Square Gardens, looked down on a riotous crowd of 20,000? But there was Andy in 1969, up there with his three only slightly older band mates in Free. A few weeks earlier, when still sixteen, he'd had to appear before a judge with a responsible elder back in England, where, struggling not to giggle, they'd sworn he'd be in bed at a certain time each night, a pre-condition in allowing a minor to travel out of the country without a parent or guardian. Now, having been strip-searched for drugs at customs and aggressively interviewed, here he was loaded with the Dutch courage of backstage Southern Comfort, facing a New York arena crammed with fans in a dangerous mood. The judge would have been appalled.

Yeah, the rock 'n' roll big time! Our first truly massive stadium crowd – and we were all totally blotto. The whole thing was on the edge of violent eruption, the crowd was going crazy and the sound system provided was so abysmal that we couldn't even hear ourselves. You can't imagine how scary that situation is. It was the first proper gig of our first American tour. Everyone was there to see Blind Faith, with Eric Clapton, Steve Winwood and Ginger Baker, and we were opening for them. In the sound check earlier in the day, we'd sort of scared ourselves with how vast the place was, so when someone backstage had introduced the Southern Comfort and we discovered how easily it went down, we really got stuck in. When the time came, there were literally as many people outside trying to get in as there already were inside filling out the arena. The riot cops were wading into people, it was all kicking off. We were on this ludicrous central revolving stage in the middle of it all, and we came on completely out of it. We probably played for no more than twenty minutes and no-one was listening to us, they just wanted Blind Faith and were going crazy. They had these shitty, weedy speakers and we could barely hear ourselves. In fact at one point Simon and I were doing one song while Paul and Koss were doing a different one and it took a while before we could hear enough to realise. I kicked a microphone off the side of the revolving stage, watched it get dragged around, then every time the stage came back past the security guy, he would conscientiously place it back up there. And I'd kick it off again. That's the kind of night it was. When Blind Faith did come out they lasted maybe one-and-a-half numbers before the stage was stormed by the fans, security guys trying in vain to keep them back while getting hit by the drumsticks Ginger was flicking at them. That was the end of *that* show. Clapton and Winwood had to be rescued. We were standing to the side watching it all, Chris Blackwell was panicking, shouting, 'We've got to save Steve, we've got to save Steve.' Clapton looked a million dollars in the middle of it all, like it was happening to someone else. Yeah, it was funny but kind of scary.

Andy talks with a casual, easy-going style, his accent a mix of English and Australian (picked up from regular contact with his Australia-based daughters) and hardly any Californian, despite having lived there for over three decades. He is far removed from the caricature of the flamboyant gay man: 'Look, I'm never going to be the dude in pink trousers waving placards from the back of a flat-bed truck! Mmm.' That little 'mmm' sound is in the meter of amused approval of an idea or image, sometimes the precursor to all-out laughter. He makes it as he describes Clapton looking regally immune from the chaos.

In everything Andy does, he's the other side of town from 'in your face' and always has been. Watch old footage of Free and there he is rocking from side to side in perfect time, but all the histrionics are from the mic-throwing singer Paul Rodgers or the big-maned guitarist Paul Kossoff in apparent agony or ecstasy as he seizes the notes from the ether and squeezes them out. Even behind the drums there's visual drama as Simon Kirke is bent forward over his kit, his long hair flailing over his face. But Andy, he just stands there gently rocking, looking to his left down the end of his bass to his band-mates, overseeing them, the measured, calm musical root even as his fingers are on a dazzling exploration of the fret board.

He's light and easy company but that calm delivery can sometimes sugar-coat cutting observations. He's precise, articulate and laser-targeted in anything he's criticising and he talks from a position of knowledge on current affairs, geo-politics and wider culture as well as the particularities of the music business. You might say he takes no shit if that didn't suggest a certain aggressive brusqueness, because there's nothing overtly aggressive about his manner, only sometimes in the message. You could miss it if you weren't listening. He'll be gone by the time you realise he's disagreeing. He doesn't do conflict so much as silent deleting. He's as strong-minded and strong-willed as you'd expect of someone who's made it from nothing and who has conquered the sort of obstacles that would defeat most of us. Calm, low-key, under-the-radar, insistent and totally independent, he's a quietly unstoppable force. There's a core of steel there but a lot of laid-back cool before you get to it. He'll give pretty much anyone the benefit of the doubt, but if that trust turns out to be misplaced, you'll cease to exist. His father, still alive, has ceased to exist since about 1970.

Hours after that New York gig, after it had all died down, as Andy, Paul Rodgers, Simon Kirke and Paul Kossoff made their way out, there were a few straggling fans. One of them said, 'Hey, you guys were better than Blind Faith.' From there to the hotel in the back of a limo, spliffs burned merrily. Just turned seventeen.

Free at this stage were a 'breaking' band, not yet in the mass public consciousness, but signed up to Chris Blackwell's Island Records and already establishing a reputation as one of the best purveyors of the emerging blues-rock sound. Their music was a beautiful but powerful take on the form, played with often startling intensity. Amid initial negotiations with Island, someone had said, 'OK, you're pretty guys, but can you play?' Rodgers' explosive response was: 'We're the best fucking blues band in the world.' When the smoke cleared the silence was broken by sixteen-year-old Andy's calm voice: 'Unless you guys realise that, we ain't signing.'

Fronted by Rodgers, standard rock god alpha male and still arguably the greatest voice in rock 'n' roll history, Free's focal point live was invariably the lion-haired guitarist Kossoff who combined a sparseness in his playing with a vibrato technique that allowed him to bend a note and sustain it like no other guitarist. He made it *sound as if his guitar was crying. To the guitar connoisseur it remains one of the most striking and recognisable sounds in music. Kirke would be bent over his drums keeping the whole thing grounded with a hard, solid backbone of a beat. It was this that allowed Fraser his unique driving style on bass, playing it in a much more creative way than in most bands where it's used simply to anchor the song. He would use it sparingly but when it came in it was as a lead instrument, pushing the song, lending it both power and traction, and always well forward in the mix, another key point of distinction in the band's sound. There was a sparse beauty about them that transcended even the songs and it was created by space. That gap between the notes summoned a tension, one that gave the sounds a power way beyond their nominal value. In an era of showman virtuosity it marked them out as different, mature, musically knowing, relaxed but with enormous implicit power that was only rarely unleashed.*

The classically trained Fraser was effectively the musical director, the one who knew how to achieve the sounds they sought. Rodgers and Fraser were the songwriting axis. As a unit they were thoroughbreds, purists, steeped in the traditions of blues and soul music. But a blues-rock band is one very macho environment. Not a good place for a gay guy so lost in the closet that he doesn't even know he's in there.

There would invariably be girls of course. There'd be so many after a gig that everyone brought one back to the hotel, and one of them would inevitably end up with me, not particularly of my choosing. I'd just be faking it thinking, 'Why not?' After all, at that age you can fuck a pillow and still get off, right? But I was never really there, never really into it, just let it happen to me really and didn't question why. To contemplate being gay at that stage would have been just so horrifically inconvenient for the band, so I buried it, denied it even to myself.

If I was honest, I had flashes of it when I was five but you completely bury it and I'm sure a lot of kids up until being teenagers experiment. For me there was definitely more but I never allowed myself to completely go there. The four of us would be driving to a gig together and we'd see someone obviously gay on the street and it was usually Simon who'd make some homophobic comment and I'd feel the hackles rise, but I'd never say anything. In fact I was probably guilty of uttering such stuff myself, such was the need to be 'one of the boys'. I've since discovered that some gay guys in therapy have even admitted to violent gay bashing, which I guess is an inner fight being externalised. At the time I wouldn't even question myself why Simon's comments created some tension in me. It was a door I just couldn't even begin to contemplate opening. Self-delusion is a very powerful thing.

The band's first two albums sold steadily and as a live act they quickly gathered a big following. But the breakthrough, in 1970, was the smash hit single 'All Right Now'. Its poppy melody was still underpinned by the band's potent sound, but it attracted a whole new audience, not just the purists. From this point on, Free were a major headline act, their booking fees quadrupled, their royalties income went stratospheric, they were on the front page of Time magazine. Because Blackwell had integrity and hadn't contractually ripped them off like most bands of the time were ripped off, they each individually became very wealthy young men, particularly the principal songwriters Rodgers and Fraser. The suddenness of this level of success for four guys not yet out of their teens made for some incongruities.

I hadn't yet learned to drive, but I'd bought this new Mercedes when we'd been touring in Germany. One of our roadies, Graham, brought it to the hotel in Amsterdam where we were appearing next, the idea being that he would then drive it to England for me. But it was in the car park next to our hotel and one afternoon I decided I'd have a go at driving it. I was telling myself, 'Come on, you can do this,' and I had a little practice in the car park. I then took it out into the street and within seconds I'd made this left-hand turn and crunched the side against a parked car. Oops! I decided I'd let Graham drive it home. Traffic were on the same bill as us and I was talking with Steve Winwood who said, 'Oh, you got some wheels,' and we both sat in the back of it smoking, getting mellow. Couldn't drive it yet, but I could sit and smoke in it at least. I passed my test in that car and had it for ages. Before I had my licence it used to just sit outside and I'd sit in it smoking joints.

Fraser at the time still lived at his mum's council house when not on the road and the image of the pint-sized, exotic-looking teenage kid in his full rock star regalia, flowing curly locks topped by flamboyant hat, pulling up in this council estate street in his brand new Mercedes is a wonderful one and somehow very much of its time, a liberating vision of how anything seemed possible, how the social order was breaking down, the staid old British guard on the way out. The Beatles had started it, but it was an order that Free, the young cutting edge of a rock aristocracy, fitted readily into.

Blackwell had such a fine-honed feel for 'now', of what was happening and hip right this minute. He saw us as part of that, had us down at Carnaby Street to get the right threads, made us get our teeth done: 'Come on. You're a star now.' I was happy to go along with it. We were together, we trusted in each other totally, took our moral compass from each other, we were creating this great music and I believed we hadn't even scratched the surface of our potential, a feeling of, 'There's the horizon, let's head for it,' that we were going for unchartered waters.

Who knows definitively why it all went wrong, why the band split apart at the seams when they had barely begun to deliver on their promise? But certainly the physical and psychological health of Kossoff was a significant contributor. Andy had already left once, then re-joined, when they were in LA, headed for The Palladium in April 1972 for the first gig of another American tour. However little Kossoff had had to do with the original split, his ailing state was very much behind the band getting back together.

After the first split the bottom line was that Koss was slipping so fast we thought re-grouping was the only way to pull him out of it. Amazing how many guitarists end up drug cases. Guitars and drugs definitely seem to go together.

We had to give him a reason for continuing on this very rapid downwards drugs slide. It seemed the only thing that might save him. Just before the American tour he gave every appearance of going straight – it looked like it was working.

We'd done a brief UK tour before we headed for LA and though Koss had given us some hairy moments then, by the time we went to the States he had us convinced this was going to be OK. He seemed straight and very much up for it. We were actually on our way to the gig and they called his room at reception, no answer. I went up there, banged on the door and shouted for him, still no answer. Eventually we got a hotel guy to break the door down. There he was, on the bathroom floor, totally out of it. We had to get an ambulance to take him to hospital. We joined him there and stayed until they assured us he was out of danger and we did the gig late, just the three of us. He'd not even made it to the first gig of the American leg. Maybe he'd just been putting on a facade all along or maybe he really had been straight but had needed something to get back on stage at such a big venue and wasn't used to it and so had over-done the dose, I don't know. But it felt like we'd turned our back for five minutes and straight away it was back to this, worse than ever in fact.

It was heart-breaking, with us all reaching out to him and him spiralling away from us regardless. How could it ever have come to this? It had all been so happening, we'd been four guys with such maturity and integrity and love for what we were doing and total respect for each other. We were set on the right course and I couldn't ever have imagined that changing. For it to end up in something you could now put in the same bracket as Spinal Tap was just beyond my wildest imagination or comprehension.

Thirty-seven years on from finding Koss on the bathroom floor, Andy tells this story from his rock star pad in Temecula, a couple of hours drive from LA, looking out across the valley that leads on to the mountains and the vineyards. His studio is upstairs and after working out for several hours each day he will religiously go up there to work, still chasing self-expression, still driven by that need, a drive that was there even when no-one else was hearing his music, in the twenty-odd year gap between his final 'straight' album and Naked And Finally Free, his coming out album of 2005.

While Rodgers formatted a sort of meat 'n' potatoes template of Free to form a band, Bad Company, that continued to bring him the success and public validation so important to him and subsequently fronted Queen, still playing to stadium audiences, Fraser is a solitary figure, who never again caught the limelight. He darts around his pad, a small bundle of energy, still chasing the future, almost dismissive of his past. To look over his shoulder, he says, feels like death. His musical legacy seems almost irrelevant to him, yet to Rodgers you get the impression it's very much part of who he is and how he sees himself. The two former partners barely communicate these days. Every so often Andy would receive an e-mail from Blackwell's publishing company asking if he was OK with Queen performing 'All Right Now' and he would reply, invariably in the positive but part of him wondering how on earth anyone could bear to try to relive their past night after night like that. That particular distinction between the two men actually underscores much of what ripped the band they so treasured apart. Later, that driving need of Andy's to be always striving, always looking for new and better ways of self-expression eventually led him to confront the hidden demon of just exactly who he really was, something that he'd unconsciously hidden from, behind the shield of his career.

Between those days when Fraser and Rodgers spearheaded 'the best blues band in the world' and now, Rodgers' life seems barely different. By contrast, for Fraser it could all have been someone else's life. He'd apparently disappeared off the face of the earth sometime in the 1980s, a major star of the early '70s simply gone from public view and forgotten – except by the legions of Free fans. Out of the public eye, this precociously gifted child star who'd never been anything other than a professional musician, who'd gone straight from childhood to stardom, by-passing adolescence, finally began to work out who he was. Where he is at now is the product of a long and deep search into himself that yielded some surprising answers but by way of some agonising processes.

ALL RIGHT NOW

The kid must have cut quite a figure as he hauled his cherry-red electric bass around the mid-60s clubs, thirteen years old, wild hair, small but perfectly formed, a carefree air of musician cool but an underlying self-control and determination. He was already being paid gig money, playing with much older musicians and earning their respect, already living the life of a young adult – once school was done for the day, at any rate. That was Andy, child prodigy, making his own way in life already, his profession established at about the same time as puberty. He never worked as anything other than a musician, never took a job in a burger bar, never stacked supermarket shelves, never worked in an office, dreaming of the day he'd be a professional musician. He simply just became one. Back home on the Roehampton council estate, 25 Horndean Close, about fifteen miles west of the London clubs he was playing, a mother no doubt fretted. The father was long gone. Andy was already the man of the house.

My father gave me one good thing – a feel for calypso music. He's from Tobago in the West Indies, the grandson of a white Scottish plantation owner and a black slave woman. The music of that place is in my blood, that reggae-like groove, that driving energy. I liked his record collection but he was a vain, arrogant, selfish, scheming, self-serving scoundrel of a man and mum was well shot of him. Not that I realised as much, aged about six, when he left. That would have made my brother Gavin about four, my sisters, Gail and Anne, five and ten. I never saw him again until I was an adult. I sought him out when we were enjoying a lot of success with Free. I wanted to see him through adult eyes, this mythical figure from childhood. We hung out for just one day, almost all of which he spent trying to convince me to take a mortgage on the cottage I'd just bought outright so I could give him the cash. I almost fell for it too. That night I lay turning it all over in my mind, then came sharply to my senses. At about 3am, I got out of bed, went to his room, woke him up and said, 'Right, you. Out, now.' I deleted him from my life. Just like he'd deleted us.

My mum was pretty and blonde, and sweet, so sweet. She worked up to three jobs to support us all but her main job was in the catering hall of the local hospital. She was conscientious, hard-working, had a lovely manner, a bit giggly, always thought the best of people – sometimes to the point of naivety maybe. I say that only in hindsight. In my teens I'd have all these musicians in the house, up in my room with the walls I'd painted purple, we'd be playing and smoking hash but she never seemed to cotton on. I laugh now thinking back; what *was* she thinking? She even caught me once on the phone scoring hash and she asked around at the hospital how one would go about curing a hash addict. When they told her that you can't really become addicted to hash, she was OK. She was lovely.

She bought me a toy piano one Christmas and I really got into it, then insisted, aged about eight, that I have a real one. She did a deal to buy one from a local pub, cost her about a fiver. She agreed on condition that I had lessons. I didn't think I needed any, of course, but agreed to it. I was taught by an old lady with a huge nose who didn't want to take me initially. She thought I was too young, that my hands wouldn't stretch far enough. I learned Beethoven and Mozart parrot-like. It felt like extra homework but actually the theory that was drilled into me then has given me an understanding that's made it far easier for me. Knowing how all the chords and keys are related makes it so much easier when you get to the stage where you're expressing yourself in music. I've worked with several great artists that haven't had that basic foundation and who have found it very difficult. When I got a guitar I worked out how the piano notes related to those on the guitar, based on that basic piano foundation. I was seen in Free as the bass player but actually that was just where I could serve the best function and my bigger role was as the band's musical director and that came from that early technical knowledge. I'd have played tambourine, or any other instrument, if that had been more helpful to the whole.

That piano was hopelessly out of tune but I loved it. It stayed in that house until well into the days of Free and I wrote the Free song 'Heavy Load' on it. What a great investment. Playing the piano, I knew I'd found home, found my thing. I guess I was fortunate to find it so young. I had no interest in anything else. My brother and his friends would be out playing football, running around, ribbing each other and I just didn't feel a part of whatever was going on out there. I was totally into this other world. Yet I was never lonely. I was sort of self-sufficient from that time, didn't feel the need for anything else, just lost in the music.

That sort of marks you out a bit at school, you know one of those kids that doesn't play football, likes music, plus there was the odd taunt of 'nigger' which is pretty laughable when you look at me even if biologically I am one-eighth black. Because I was smaller than most of the others too, I became a bit of a punching bag, especially at junior school. I graduated to senior school, a place called St Clement Danes, where my elder sister Anne had already been for five years. She suffered from a condition related to when she'd contracted meningitis as a child of about six months. They were living out in British Guyana and because of the times and the place it wasn't handled properly and it led her to becoming epileptic. The medicine for that in those days was very crude and it completely changed her personality. She'd been this incredibly bright kid but it basically retarded everything about her, made her very hard to relate to. So she'd been bullied at school, and when I arrived as her brother I inherited a bit of that too. I'd decided I'd had enough of this one day and when the tough guy came to pick on me I split his face open. It was weird, he shrunk down to nothing. This kid that had seemed so tough suddenly seemed very small. We became half-friendly afterwards but on my terms and I sort of psychologically dominated him. I thought I will not be beaten now by anyone and the bigger the challenge the better. From that moment I never had any more trouble with bullying and it allowed me to become a lot more sociable.

I became part of a little group of 'arty' kids and we formed a band, played in break times at school. We all had guitars and everyone wanted to be the guitarist or the singer. No-one wanted to be the bassist, it just wasn't cool. So I, ever the diplomat, agreed to do it. I tuned the strings of my Airstream Lucky 7 guitar down an octave and voila, a bass! It must've sounded terrible, but to a twelve-year-old it was all pretty cool. We played Wilson Pickett numbers, mainly. I later graduated to a proper bass guitar.

At around this time Anne was going out with a guy called Binky McKenzie. He was a bass player, one hell of a bass player, maybe the most amazing bass player of all time.

Binky McKenzie was a black phenomenon who had already worked with such established and serious artists as Alexis Korner, John McLaughlin and Denny Laine, among others. He was a wild man, and not of the 'loveable rogue'-type either, but with a very dark side that would eventually lead to his imprisonment for murder. At this time however his drug intake wasn't so bad – he was not as uncontrollable as he would later become.

Anne would bring him round the house and I'd leave my bass lying around in the hope that he'd play it and I could listen. People often recall a bass solo I did on the Free song 'Mr Big'. Well, take that and multiply it by about 10 and keep it that level all the time and that was how good Binky was. In fact that solo of mine came to me pretty much from memory flashbacks of the sort of thing Binky was doing when he was round our place. But to my mind it was a pretty pale imitation. He could do blues, soul, jazz, anything. There was a buzz about him; everyone was saying, 'This is the guy.' He was set to be the next big superstar musician, a genius.

He'd play and I'd listen in through the door or ear against the wall. But he'd never show me anything, he guarded his skills very jealously, which is something I just never got. But he did help a little, with suggestions about some people he knew over in Willesden who he'd heard were looking for a bass player. Turned out one of them was his brother Bunny, a much more easy-going character than Binky. I went over to Binky's place to meet with them and after trying out we got together. Binky's and Bunny's father was some sort of musician too and there'd always be the sounds of BB King or Muddy Waters permeating the air. This was much more of a black part of town and these guys were very much into blues, rhythm and blues and ska. This was my first real exposure to this music and I got into it in a big way. Playing with these guys in the black clubs as a very young white kid I was looked upon as a bit of a novelty I suppose. They'd have been in their early twenties, I was still only thirteen or so but I really didn't notice that age difference. It felt natural for me to seek out musicians that were at the same stage as me and I don't think it seemed strange to them either.

I guess, looking back, there may have been an element of me being the man of the house that led me to getting out there straight away. By definition I was the man of the house, and there was no father figure there to say, 'No, you can't do that.' But it never felt like a burden. I was certainly very aware of my mother's plight. She was doing three jobs a day and it certainly felt good to be able to put some money on the table. It all happened very naturally, I just did it, but while it allowed me to develop musically at a very fast rate, maybe it denied me an adolescence. That's not something I ever gave a moment's thought to until much later in life, when I was struggling with my sexual identity. Maybe if I'd had a more conventional adolescence I'd have experimented a bit and found out who I really was, maybe it somehow enabled the repression, I don't know.

The transition from child to adult was sudden, I guess, and I'm not sure if that was because the music pulled me that way or whether being independent so early allowed me to pursue the music opportunities. At one point, at quite a young age, I recall telling Mum that I wasn't coming to church with her. She used to drag us down there but she only seemed to be religious on Sunday mornings to me. I wasn't buying into that. You get to a certain age and just say, 'I'm not going, I've got other stuff to do.' In a sense I discounted God because of that whole negative experience. But much later I'd have cause to re-think.

At first Binky was a pretty normal sort of guy though he always had a bit of a chip on his shoulder, being maybe not as big as he would have liked and black. He was a bit intense, sort of a Wesley Snipes-type of guy, a tough little nugget, kind of smooth and very determined. But as he got more heavily into drugs so he changed. He became a bit crazy. I used to leave my amp at the place of the guitarist, a guy called Christopher Harding. Binky developed a habit of going around there and just taking my amp when he needed it. One day Christopher – who was way bigger than Binky – told him that he really shouldn't be doing that and Binky threatened him in such a way that he left town immediately and joined the merchant navy. We never heard from him again. Binky was developing into a very dark character. I guess Christopher had seen that this was a potential murderer threatening him. He definitely had it in him by this time.

Shortly afterwards Binky McKenzie murdered his parents and a policeman with his bare hands. He was sentenced to life imprisonment and remains behind bars to this day.

I was also in another band called The Lawless Breed at around this time, based in Battersea, a bit closer to where I lived. I replied to an ad for that one.

We were a covers band, doing Wilson Pickett, Otis Redding, Sam and Dave, The Supremes. I'd only need to hear 'In The Midnight Hour' once to be able to play the bass part, it wasn't like I was developing my own style at this point. The singer in this band, Sid, was black. He saw himself as a sort of James Brown, would dance and strut around like him. They were late-teens/early twenties. We'd play in small clubs mainly, a few army bases. We opened for Amen Corner once. I recall a place called Tiles in London on Oxford Street. There was a place in Fulham where we'd do five sets a night. Orange silk shirts, very cool!

Sid had a van that was forever breaking down and we would barely break even after we'd fixed whatever had caused the latest inevitable mechanical calamity. Sometimes I'd catch the bus instead or miss the last one home. God knows what I put my mother through. In that band we found a sax player from somewhere north of Scarborough, a great guy and a great horn player, Arthur. He'd bring his mate Albert who was the funniest, looniest guy you could ever meet. He was at his funniest when he was drunk and kept us in stitches. He ended up looking after Steve Winwood's arrangements and was very loyal to him. Years later in a strange circle of events I hooked back up with him, a wonderful guy.

You'd imagine that all the late nights playing in bands would have played havoc with my school life but I actually don't think it did. I was still getting pretty good grades. I only really started having a problem at school when I got very influenced by the look of The Beatles as they went into their psychedelic phase and I grew my hair. The deputy head took exception to this. He was quite a piece of work. You'd see him coming down the corridor and with his long flowing gown swishing behind him like he was Dearth Vader – kids would be scattering off in all directions to avoid him because whoever he saw he would make their life hell, a truly awful man. So he had it in for me and my long hair and despite my perfectly good grades I was expelled after refusing to have it cut. It would have been the first step to breaking my spirit, to making me into a good little bank clerk. I wasn't having it!

That's Andy freeze-framed right there, a stubborn free spirit with plenty of his own discipline and no need for anyone else's. Beneath that easy-going exterior, he can be immovable on matters of principle or self-determination. Maybe it's something to do with having grown up so quick then moved into an environment that celebrates the spurning of authority. More likely, it's just him and probably one of the reasons why he made it so quickly.

KORNERED BY FATE

I broke the good news to mum and naturally she was very concerned, so to placate her I went off to Hammersmith College of Further Education to study art. This was 1967, I was fifteen. It relieved mum's anxieties but all I learned there really was how to roll a good joint. Jimi Hendrix would be blasting through the common room and I recall seeing Chicken Shack perform there at our Christmas party. I met a girl, Sappho Korner. She was the daughter of Alexis Korner, the jazz musician. But at that time I'd no idea who he was. Sappho was a bit of a wild child, a party girl, very cute, looked sort of like a young Katie Couric. We became an item and for a few months it was a pretty serious relationship. She was never focussed intellectually, I think she wanted to be Bessie Smith or Billie Holiday, wanted to sing and tried to. Maybe she could have succeeded if she'd focussed herself but that was just not in her. In the end – much later – she thought being a heroin addict would do it. And it didn't. But for a time it was pretty good. I remember she had a very good looking older friend with an even older boyfriend and the four of us had a hell of a time under the sheets.

I began to spend a lot of time at Sappho's place and they were such an open, friendly family that they just sort of invited me to be a part of it and that's when I got to know Alexis. He was a wonderful guy, very easy to know, very relaxed, smoking Gauloises and joints galore, inviting me to join him. I started off going there to see Sappho but increasingly I'd spend more time with her dad, who became sort of a father figure to me, I guess.

Andy could not have stumbled into a more fortuitous contact if he'd planned it. Alexis Korner was arguably the single most influential man on the British blues scene. He truly was 'The Daddy'. Of mixed Greek and Austrian parentage, raised in France, Switzerland and North Africa before arriving in London at eleven, he was thirty-nine years old by the time his daughter introduced him to Andy and could have been mistaken for his father, especially in his musician's garb and afro hair.

Since breaking out on his own after serving as a member of the Chris Barber Jazz Band, he had, as a musician and proprietor of the London Blues and Barrelhouse Club in Soho in the 1950s and early 60s, been hugely influential in the popularisation of blues music in Britain. He and his partner Cyril Davies, as well as fronting a standard-setting blues band, also brought to the UK some of the original American blues greats, and their influence on a whole generation of impressionable young British musicians was profound. The Rolling Stones were aided immeasurably by Korner's early patronage and they tell stories of returning to Korner's house after a performance, climbing through his kitchen window and discovering the Muddy Waters band asleep on the floor.

By the time Andy met him, Korner's blues-jazz band Blues Incorporated had fizzled out and he now occupied the role of 'elder statesman', though he still performed. It would be difficult to think of someone better connected in the world Andy aspired to.

One of the musicians who had dived into the 'British blues boom' that Korner had helped create was John Mayall, a blues guitarist from Manchester. It had actually been Korner who had persuaded him, in the early '60s, to head south for London and become a full-time musician even though he was already in his early thirties. Korner helped get him started, arranging gigs and introductions and in no time John Mayall's Bluesbreakers were a major attraction on the British blues circuit. Initially his bass player was John McVie, later to find fame and fortune as the 'Mac' in Fleetwood Mac. He then recruited a young guitarist called Eric Clapton whose playing created a stir and set him on his way to stardom. When Clapton left, Mayall replaced him with another unknown, Peter Green, who if anything perhaps even surpassed Clapton's virtuosity and would later team up with McVie as part of Fleetwood Mac. Another who later lent his name and skills to Fleetwood Mac, Mick Fleetwood, served as The Bluesbreakers' drummer. When McVie left he was replaced by the house bassist of Ronnie Scott's Jazz Club, a fiery young guy called Jack Bruce. But within a few months Bruce too had moved on, and would later show up as bassist in a new band Cream that also featured Clapton. You get the idea of what a small and incestuous world it all was and of just what a hot-bed of talent Mayall's band was. It was early 1968 and Mayall had a European tour all booked up, but he'd just sacked his latest bassist. So he did what he usually did when he needed help – he phoned Alexis.

I was actually around with Alexis when his phone rang. I heard him say, 'Well, I've got this guy hangs around with my daughter who says he is a bass player – and I think he probably is. Could give him a try, I suppose.' Mayall needed a new bass player like yesterday. It was a Friday and John only lived a few streets away so we went around there over the weekend, John played a few 12-bar blues numbers – all very standard – and I played bass. It wasn't exactly stretching stuff, just basic blues. John said, 'Yep, great. We need to go out Monday and get you a better bass and a stereo system, get you some sounds,' and that's what we did. The rest of that week I had my hands full quitting college in a hurry, getting a passport and working visas – because the following week we were playing in Europe. So I was in court, getting the judges to allow me to work abroad because I was only fifteen. That was my first experience of that little charade – the accompanying adult swearing to the magistrate that I'd be in bed by eight: 'We'll make sure he doesn't indulge in any untoward behaviour etc. etc.' Yeah, right. I think we were out to Holland on the Thursday.

I also had to explain to Mum, of course. She was initially somewhat aghast – you know: 'You're leaving school *again*? You're joining a *group*?' But I think she was swayed by the money and the idea that this was a proper professional band. We hadn't been making any money with The Lawless Breed and I would be on a regular good wage with Mayall – £50 a week, an absolute fortune at the time. John in fact ran a very tight ship. He was the boss, the rest of us were his employees. He may have looked like the biggest stoner around but he was anything but. He was a straight cornflakes-in-the-morning sort of guy and ran the band very much as a business, always knowing exactly how much was coming in and going out. He certainly did not approve of any weed-taking and I would have to nip off out of sight with the guitarist Mick Taylor for that. If Mayall had caught us I'm pretty sure we would have been fired.

Mick became a great friend. He was only three years older than me so we could relate. We were in Amsterdam and were sharing a joint once and I went back to my room and lay on the bed and was suddenly conscious of all the blood in all the veins in my body moving towards a raging hard-on! I was like, 'Wow! What an experience!' and I went back to Mick and tried to explain it and he just looked at me kind of askance and said, 'Dude, you're really stoned.' You'd think it would have taken acid to do something like that but this was just from hash.

Mick was the one I was closest to but everyone was very decent, though the drummer Keef Hartley really didn't take to me at all for some reason. Maybe I had creases in my pants or something, I don't know! I just somehow rubbed him up the wrong way. I bumped into him in later years because he was in various groups that opened for Free and it was all cool by then. But I definitely got the impression during the Mayall time that he sort of wished I wasn't there. He was a really solid drummer; I've no idea what he thought of my playing. I tend to like to go places with the bass, something that requires the drummer to stay really tight and solid, and maybe that left him with nowhere to go but I can't imagine it was that because it was just 12-bar blues. John would just call out the key and the tempo and that was it. How hard could it be? It was either fast or slow.

These were mature adult professional players and I had nothing to do but learn. The drums and bass were supposed to be back and solid and others would take turns at solos. Mick – who was the star guitarist, a terrific player and who later joined the Rolling Stones – and one of the horn players would take turns at the solos. I was probably a bit over-dressed for the Bluesbreakers.

I'd picked up some of my dress sense from Alexis, who was a very extrovert dresser and some from Jimi Hendrix. I wasn't with them long enough for them to grind me down to jeans and sneakers.

Our first tour took in Holland, Germany and a few dates in France, I think. All were in pretty decent-sized theatre places. It was all a bit of a whirlwind. We toured in Mayall's van, a long Transit with his bed across the top behind the seats and a load of foam on the floor for the rest of us. We continued with that when we got back to England. If we had a gig in Leeds he'd take us all home that night, drop everyone off, drop me at my mother's at about three in the morning.

It lasted only about six weeks all told, but it had been a great experience. John told me and Keef that he was looking for more of a jazz direction and got Tony Reeves and John Hiseman, players more of that ilk. Maybe that was the simple truth or maybe he felt there's some kind of rift between these guys and it ain't working, I don't know. It didn't even faze me. I wasn't married to the band. It was his trip, I was way too young to have any serious commitments, those things that adults get burdened with, and so just said, 'Yeah, OK.'

So I went back to hanging out at Alexis's place and he'd have me along playing in his band at gigs here and there. It must have been a very difficult period for Sappho. We were becoming less of an item but here I was still around all the time, with her dad helping me and opening all kinds of doors for me. I'm sure that must have put her through all sorts of heavy changes.

One of the things Alexis suggested for me was to get in touch with a guitar player called Paul Kossoff who was in a band that was already up to their fifteenth bass player or something. Alexis had been talking to the producer Mike Vernon and it came from that conversation. I didn't find out until many, many years later, way after Free, that Koss and Simon had gone to a gig I was doing with Mayall to check me out, to see if I was worth bothering with, I guess.

Vernon, as well as being a producer, also had his own label and club and so was well tuned in to emerging talent. He knew that Kossoff and Simon Kirke, the guitarist and drummer, were thinking of quitting the band Black Cat Bones to set something up with the vocalist from Brown Sugar, Paul Rodgers. Vernon was friendly with all three and knew they'd rehearsed but were struggling to find a bass player. Hence his call to Korner who informed him he had just the man. Korner later spoke directly to Kirke in recommending Fraser. Just the fact that Andy was playing with Mayall got the attention of Kirke, Kossoff and Rodgers. But on being told Andy had just been sacked by Mayall and was on his last few gigs, Kirke was dubious. When he then found he was only fifteen he was doubly so. But, on Korner's recommendation, he and Kossoff went down to a 51 Club gig in London's Leicester Square where the Mayall band, with Andy still on bass, were playing. Kirke's doubts were further fuelled when his first impression of the exotically dressed Fraser as he walked to the stage was that of 'a little fairy boy'. 'Well, this was the '60s and everyone dressed more flamboyantly,' says Kirke today, 'but yeah, he did look a bit effeminate. But Jesus, he started playing and we were all knocked sideways. He took a solo that I still recall to this day, he was incredible. Plus, he exuded confidence and seemed to be enjoying himself. We forgot all about how he was dressed from that moment and it never again crossed my mind that he might have been gay.'

Not only did I not know they were there but I only found out very recently that Simon's first impression of me that night was that I was gay. In which case he knew about twenty years before I did! I think very often first impressions are accurate, undiluted by any subsequent knowledge or experience. I find it absolutely fascinating that that was his first impression. More recently a gardener who worked for me for many years told me he'd absolutely just assumed I was gay on first meeting me and had then thought no more about it, yet at that time I still hadn't realised I was. So clearly others could see it and I couldn't. I also recall once overhearing, when I was about ten, my mother talking about a gay person at work and she said if ever one of her sons turned out queer she'd kill them. I don't know if there was something in me she saw that made her suspect I might be gay and so was talking out loud to me or not – but it really had an impact on me.

I actually met Koss for the first time when he came over to my mother's house and we jammed together. He turned up in his Morris Minor Traveller. He had this amazing look with that lion's mane hair and cheeky little face. He was also about the same size as me, i.e. fairly small, as were the others. That was just one of so many ways in which we were well matched. After our jamming session Koss suggested that the four of us get together. We met up the following week at the Nag's Head in Battersea.

That pub was where Vernon's jazz club Blue Horizon was based. Kossoff arrived first to meet up with Vernon who unlocked the upstairs function room he had arranged the band rent from the Nag's landlord. It was April 19, 1968. Andy, still not yet sixteen, was the last to arrive. He climbed from the taxi cab impressing Kirke and Rodgers – who'd just arrived by bus – enormously, especially when he asked for a receipt. He was, after all, a 'name' – he'd played with John Mayall; he was big time. After wrestling his amp out of the cab he shook hands with the others and they walked up the stairs to their destiny. Free had just been born.

ALL RIGHT NOW

The story of what transpired that Friday afternoon in the room above the bar in The Nag's Head has since acquired mythical status. Some sort of musical osmosis occurred as four exceptional individuals somehow melded into one very special unit. They started with a few blues standards but soon enough were creating new songs, several of which would end up on their first album a few months later. Kossoff and Kirke had worked together for the previous year or so but Rodgers had only ever rehearsed with them and Andy was new to all of them. But it sparked instantly; they each began playing off the energy of the others, spurring each other to new heights. This was evident not only in their playing but also on a creative level. Something extraordinary was brewing here.

The room was small and we barely even fitted onto the stage, but it was empty and it hadn't cost us much. We jammed for a couple of hours and immediately it felt very, very good, happening, fresh, no brain strain at all. Although Koss was the one who struck you first – it was always that way with anyone who saw us live – it didn't take long at all for me to realise that actually everyone here was *really* strong. Paul Rodgers had the most fabulous voice, Koss was interacting with that really well in what he was playing, Simon's drumming was fantastically grounded and solid, such a fantastic timekeeper that I was able to feel free to let go on the bass, that the whole thing wouldn't collapse if I wasn't in tight with the kick drum. We started really good and it just got better from there. By the end of the two hours, there was definitely a 'Wow' feeling.

Actually, it was Alexis's fortieth birthday and there was a party for him nearby. I'd been telling him all about this lion-haired guitarist I'd jammed with and that he should come down and see and he said he would try – and he did for about the last fifteen minutes. He definitely got it, absolutely felt what we'd felt, realised we were onto something pretty special.

Not only did Korner get it, he immediately called his agent/manager Bryan Morrison. Korner decided he was going to have them as his opening act and they would subsequently sign with the Bryan Morrison Agency, an agreement that covered publishing, recording and management as well as gigs. After a time supporting Korner, honing their act, they began to venture out on their own.

The thing that really made it feel unique was how we all gave each other space in our playing. That really stood out for me and it lent the whole sound a great power and spirit. It's something I see in the great orators. You watch Barack Obama for example, and everything comes from silence. It starts off and you can hear a pin drop, that space in between is everything so that anything you add then has a big effect. A good speaker knows this, knows how to command silence; they begin softly and so when they start saying things with vigour it becomes incredibly powerful. We had that with Free, just naturally fell into that from the very first moment. Although people say they would love to hear Free together now, aside from the fact that Koss isn't with us any more, it could never be the same anyway because although everyone was talented, the most important thing was the spirit and what was in between the notes. That was derived from the respect we had for each other and the joint vision, how we each understood, without it being said, what we were trying to do. If you heard us now and there was no spirit you'd realise there were just some very simple riffs that didn't mean much without spirit.

We might've been playing it cool afterwards but we all realised what we'd got here. I don't think we even sought agreement that it was happening, we all just sort of acknowledged it was. Then we were talking about what we should call ourselves. Alexis had a band once called Free At Last and it was him who suggested taking just part of that and calling ourselves Free. That one-word summary of a spirit was quite in at the time and we'd all been quite influenced by Cream, so it all sort of made sense. Paul Rodgers has said we went into that room as four individuals and came out of it a couple of hours later a band, and I'd go along with that.

Once we'd agreed a name, I then said, 'OK, I'm the leader, then.' I'm sure they thought, 'Who the fuck is this guy coming in and saying that?' I'm not quite sure today why I said that, maybe youthful ignorance, cockiness, maybe having come from John Mayall and having seen how he operated, organised things and knew how things had to be done. The others just humoured me basically – and did for a few years!

The thing was, we each had something to contribute. It was no particular strain for me to organise things, to get the money sorted with the gig promoters. I'd learned all that stuff from Mayall, so I figured I could serve a useful function here. I was the go-between with the band and the promoter. I'd go in there with a massive roadie behind me, his presence implying, 'You better keep the kid happy,' – an unbeatable combination really. There was hardly ever a problem and the few times there was we'd use Rodgers' verbal northern aggression to lash out at them and put them straight. If we'd gone down well I'd negotiate a better fee in advance for next time. I wouldn't say I was running the band, but I sort of took responsibility for it operationally. Later, I took a similar role between the band and Island and would pay out the wages from the gigs and do the banking, making sure we were always straight. Musically, I had an idea of where I thought we should be heading and knew how to achieve the sounds. But really there were no wallflowers in that band, we could each hold our own, no problem. We were very equally matched.

Alexis was incredibly supportive during this time, just very gracious. He'd bring us with him, give us a big build-up, tell the audience they were going to be hearing a lot more from us in the future and we'd generally get a good reception. We'd do the clubs around London but also further afield. I don't specifically remember our first gig – apparently it was in Chesterfield – but I do remember places like Rambling Jack's Blues Club in Bishops Stortford and its tiny stage. We'd incorporate quite a few blues standards into our act there, things like BB King's 'Waiting On You' and 'Rock Me Baby'.

I recall playing at the very dungeon-like Middle Earth in London along with Pink Floyd. They didn't sound anything like what they later developed into and just sort of rambled on directionless, very dark and psychedelic.

We did a gig at The Marquee in London supporting Albert King and that was such a big deal for us. Koss had turned us all onto him and we were massive fans. After our set he said something like, 'Man you boys can play the blues,' which thrilled us all but Koss was especially buzzed.

Koss had his Minor Traveller and that's what we'd use to get around and there was a bit of room in the back for our gear. Koss was the only driver at that time. We were young and carefree, every day an adventure, complete confidence that things would happen for us.

Paul and I were writing loads of stuff at this time. We'd start out with maybe a new idea for a song each day and then, when we'd built a few up, we'd whittle them down with our quality control. Alexis might offer an opinion or two in that process.

As far as my bass playing was concerned, I was not truly aware of how my style began to develop. I still have difficulty with taking myself out of that. I've never really considered myself a bass player, it was just something that was easy. I'd started on piano and wanted to then go to guitar but in Free I just did what I thought was appropriate to what we were trying to achieve in terms of feel and sound. In some Free songs I don't even come in until half way through. I only had to make it work and if that meant staying out, that was fine by me. I wasn't doing anything other than trying to be appropriate and it's always a bit of a shock for me to hear people talk about my style as a bass player. I suppose the Caribbean blood in me may have pushed me towards a more distinctive way of playing – and Simon's superb timekeeping allowed me the scope to do that – but it's not something I was aware of.

But I was aware of my development in songwriting. It wasn't something I'd done before but I learned a lot from Paul Rodgers who was already well into that process lyrically. He really opened the door to lyric-writing for me. I would help finish his songs melodically and I would have musical ideas that he would put lyrics to. I think we learned from each other and pretty soon we were both completing songs by ourselves, though in these early days Paul was probably doing more than me. Koss and Simon contributed too but in the main it was PR and me.

Paul Rodgers has written some of my favourite songs of all time and his two sides were very well expressed in Free. On the one hand, he's the northern macho man, very earthy, aggressive, not saying much, the Clint Eastwood of rock. On the other he's a sort of folk balladeer, very sensitive and that gave us some beautiful haunting melodies. I used to think of him as a lonely soldier boy on a misty battlefield, dead all around him, but going on, unstoppable but very melancholic. I thought that was a wonderful side to him, and I really hoped we'd see more of it.

In many ways we were diametrically opposed, we were the two extremes of the group dynamically. He was aggressive, take no shit. I was the opposite. I think part of what made it all work was that when two polar opposites found common ground, it could be world-inclusive, which is a long way to understanding mass appeal. Paul was very hard-working, very driven, possibly a little narcissistic. Outsiders frequently found him 'difficult' but I didn't experience this until much later. I saw him use verbal aggression just as a tool sometimes, when something needed to be done, but I always sensed it was just a stance he adopted and it wasn't directed inwards to us but to outsiders, for the band's benefit. We were competitive with each other, but in a healthy way, pushing each other, driving the other one on. I felt as close to him as a brother. If I was the mind of the band, Paul R was the voice – and what a voice. For me, we couldn't have had a more appropriate singer.

Koss was the band's soul. The guitar is the emotion in a band anyway, but he put so much emotion into it yet he never over-powered the sound, he was sympathetic and complementary to it. He played from a heart that was forever on his sleeve, and that really touches people. He had this fantastic vibrato technique, so good that even Eric Clapton asked him how he did it once – really made Koss's day, that. He struggled with chords, didn't see himself as that sort of player, was more of a blues player and yet he was trained in classical guitar and could play it beautifully. You'd hear him playing all this lovely classical stuff, just doodling and I'd say, 'Hey, that's great,' and he'd say, 'No it's not, it's crap. Right, what we doing?' and he just wouldn't acknowledge it. He seemed to find it difficult to link up all the different elements, but he did what he did brilliantly well. He was a fantastic character and definitely the funny man of the band, an incredible sense of humour but using that to keep the truth front and centre the way a good satirist does. He'd go into all these different characters and make a running commentary on the rest of us or what was happening outside and he'd have us in stitches. Because the weather was so cold in England he'd often be wearing this long grey overcoat and he'd use that to go into this sort of *Coronation Street* mean old woman character, berating the rest of us, taking the piss, very funny. But he'd also use that character to cut to the quick, in a hilarious way. I loved him for that. There was an intense integrity about Koss that set a standard for the rest of us to maintain. It included a general and a musical integrity. He hated anything he saw as not authentic and you could get him on a real riff about it. You just needed to mention Marc Bolan and T Rex and he'd be off on one! If ever anyone played anything that sounded even vaguely like Bolan, he'd be there: 'That sounds like fuckin' Marc Bolan! Away with that!' Unless things passed muster with all of us, they were rejected.

Once when we were all in the car coming back from a gig, Simon was driving and Paul R was in the front with him, me and Koss in the back. PR had some gripe with Koss and was really verbally laying into him. Meanwhile Koss was just rummaging around in his bag, not seeming to take any notice. Rodgers was still going on as Koss found what he was looking for – a mirror. He put on the interior light and held the mirror to Paul's face. It was hilarious and even Paul saw the funny side of it. Koss could easily have been a comic actor – or a Formula One driver. He was a brilliant driver, very fast but effortless, you always felt totally safe with him, that he was always 100% in control. I never felt totally comfortable with Rodgers at the wheel – nothing ever happened but I always had the feeling that he had the potential to do something wrong.

Simon, as well as being such an amazingly solid drummer, was the body or backbone of the band. He had an ability to see all three different points of view – and you couldn't get three more different personalities than Rodgers, Koss and me – and somehow unify it all. In a sense his drumming did that but he performed the same role off stage. He wasn't ever a wild guy – although like all of us he had his moments – and spoke with a very proper British accent. He's a very straight down the path sort of guy, always pulling the dynamic back to sanity, very easy-going, friendly with everyone, impossible to dislike. He also had a good voice, albeit a bit choir boy-like, and you can hear him in many of Free's backing vocals. He played pretty competent guitar and bass too.

Many years later, in '94, I played a gig at Woodstock with Paul Rodgers. The drummer was Jason Bonham. Within seconds of us starting I had the thought, 'This guy doesn't hold it down tight enough,' and my whole job became to grab hold of the rhythm, to keep him solid. I felt there was no way I could let go, or do anything creative otherwise the time would wobble. It hit me like a ton of bricks, 'Whoah!' – suddenly that was my mission. I've since seen him play in Foreigner and he didn't appear to be wobbly at all, sounded very solid and maybe it was the bass player holding him down then too. But whatever it was, I suddenly valued even more what Simon had given us all those years ago.

The biggest thing though was the group dynamic that resulted between all these different individual qualities. It sounds clichéd to say it was us against the world but it was very intense and we definitely felt on a shared mission. We were young, on an adventure, watching each other's back and we had enough between us to make up for any individual deficiencies. We had it all covered. It was a great time, on the road all the time, always in each other's company. I loved it. We had the deepest respect for each other. The teenage years are such an important growth period in your life anyway and it was at this time we came to form our values, our view on the world, our sense of social consciousness, integrity – and we got all of that from each other. It was a very, very crucial time in our lives and it was part of what made that band very special. At the time it was the love of my life and I'm pretty sure all the others felt that way too.

There's something achingly tragic about that, about how the extra intensity of youth, before it's been annealed by experience, set up an idealistic standard that subsequently proved impossible to live up to. It made the whole thing terribly brittle and in due course the unit could not withstand the awful conflicts resultant from stardom, money, artistic endeavour, opposing creative pulls and Kossoff's ultimate weakness. But in the brief period the original band existed, the combination of the individual talents and its powerful integrity – deeply earnest beneath the underlying hashish mellowness – carried upon the delicate bubble of the times, created something approaching sonic perfection. If you had the ears for it. That intense camaraderie, the shared values and complementary skills, underscored by ambition, made them a fiercely independent unit. Blackwell would later say they were 'like four points of a compass, facing north, east, south and west, their backs to each other as a force.'

But they were too young to take the rough with the smooth, too young for compromise, too young to accept imperfection, too young to listen to anyone but each other. It was what made them great but it would be the undoing of them, long before the wider world ever realised just how special they were. From that first time in the Nag's Head to somewhere just before 'All Right Now' – a period of about two years, the beginning of which Andy is talking about here – it was idyllic, an impossible standard for idealists such as these.

Some find it difficult to see what all the fuss was about. They look at footage of Free and can't see past the clichés – Rodgers throwing the mic stand about, Koss making his faces as he squeezes the notes out, the 'ooh baby' and 'huh' of Rodgers between the lyrics. But that's to look from the wrong end of the telescope. They weren't clichés then, they've become so since. Free informed the aesthetic of a whole generation of bands in the '70s, bands with similar raw power but nothing like their artistic breadth or subtlety – and from the perspective of now, Free unfortunately get lumped in with them. Listen to the songs, the minor key masterpieces of melancholy and growling, restrained power, de-sensitise your ears and eyes from what's happened in music since and you might begin to understand what producer and sometime Dylan band member Al Kooper meant when he boldly declared, 'Free is the greatest band that ever lived.'

It was quickly apparent that our manager Bryan Morrison didn't share our sense of destiny. I seemed to be booking more of our gigs than he was but, worse than that, he began begrudging the advances we needed from time to time just to stay operating. He'd put in about £400 and six months in was starting to ask when he was going to see some return and at that point we thought, 'Time to move on.' It was complicated a little by the fact that we'd done a few quick demos for him and he used these to help him hang onto the publishing rights. He was the sort of guy that placed a lot of importance on his driving a Rolls-Royce and his address of '1 Star Street' but he was kind of small-minded. I believe he let Pink Floyd and a few others slip through his fingers for similar reasons.

I spoke to Alexis about the situation and, as ever, he was cool with it. He said he would try and work out something else. He came back and said he'd arranged a meeting for us with Chris Blackwell of Island Records. He'd just got in touch with Blackwell and told him, 'You need to hear these guys.' Alexis was so well known and respected within the British music industry that when he said something like that people listened. We all went round to the Island offices, met Blackwell and it wasn't even like we were having to do a sales pitch, it was a no-sweat thing. After about five minutes we were all just assuming this was it – and so did he. We had a cup of tea and shook on it.

Although Andy and the others didn't realise it, they didn't need to sell themselves to Blackwell – because he'd seen them perform already. 'Alexis had suggested I should catch them at The Marquee when they supported Albert King. I went there with Alexis and a big blues fan called James Hamilton,' recalls Blackwell. The subsequent meeting was evidently just to check them out in person.

Shortly afterwards, Blackwell arranged that they perform a sample gig exclusively for him and his three-man Island management team – Johnny Glover, Muff Winwood and Alec Leslie – at Studio 51. Glover recalls the day well: 'Island was then at 155

Oxford Street and Blackwell one day just said to us, "Come on, there's a band I want you to see," and we walked down there to Leicester Square. It was a tiny room, I don't think it could've been more than thirty-foot square. Paul Rodgers and his microphone were about two inches in front of my face. The band was all set up, ready to go as soon as we sat down. They put on a set of four or five songs but they did it full-on, like it was a proper gig, Rodgers swinging the microphone, Koss showing his angst. It was a very aggressive show. We walked back and Blackwell looked at us. Muff was the most senior of us and he said, "No, I don't fancy it," and I said, "They were a bit in your face, Chris, a bit full-on, very aggressive," and said I didn't really fancy it either and Alec agreed.'

Then aged thirty, Blackwell was a dynamic music entrepreneur. He'd founded Island Records nine years earlier in Jamaica, where his family was then living, then had been struck by how big an export market the UK – with its large community of Jamaican migrants – proved to be. He relocated to London and the chart success of the Millie Small record 'My Boy Lollipop' launched Blackwell into the big time. Since then he had branched out into the burgeoning rock scene, initially with the Steve Winwood-fronted Spencer Davis Group. The Winwood brothers – Steve and bassist Muff – had then left that band, Steve to form the Island-contracted Traffic, Muff to become an A&R man for Island.

By mid-68, with Fairport Convention, Jethro Tull and others having already joined Traffic on the Island roster, Blackwell saw Free as an ideal addition. He was a svengali figure, but an impeccably principled one. In an era when record companies contractually ripping off their artists was the norm, Blackwell nurtured the talent, gave them fair deals. He also had his own strong ideas of the image and look his artists should have, and would often still double up as a producer even as Island was expanding. As with Korner, and in this case thanks to Korner, Andy and the band had met with exactly the right person at exactly the right time to take them to the next level.

Blackwell was so much the right guy for us. We were so lucky. I don't think even Alexis knew the extent to which that turned out to be true. Within our first meeting, even before we'd signed anything, he'd said he would arrange an out for us with Bryan Morrison and allocate money to get us a van and get some clothes, get our teeth done etc. Island wasn't like other record companies, it was more like a family and you fitted in there or you didn't.

If Blackwell had been bowled over by seeing them play, he was even more so once he'd met them in person, but was very aware of their extreme youth. They would need to be handled carefully. 'Andy was the youngest yet he was the clear leader,' recalls

Blackwell of the meeting. 'They were all very sure of themselves but Andy spoke for them. I had maximum respect for him immediately, despite his age. I came to love this band and feel like they were my kids almost. Musically, Paul Rodgers was an incredible singer with a strong blues feel, Kossoff had an amazing look and all of them were excellent musicians.'

Glover: 'I don't know if it was the next day after the Studio 51 show – it may even have been later that afternoon – Chris asked me to pop along to the office. So I go in there and there's the four of them sitting on the sofa opposite Chris! He mustn't have liked our vote and had decided we were having them anyway! He said, "We're taking the band on, we're buying out their contract and you're looking after them." Paul Rodgers looked me up and down and said, "So you didn't want to take us on, then?" and I didn't know what to say; it was very awkward. Later on I said to Chris, "Thanks for that," and he just laughed and said, "You'll love them."'

Bryan Morrison snapped up Blackwell's offer to buy the rights to the band and the time came for the contracts to be done. This time in the Island offices, in addition to Blackwell, sat the management team. This was when Muff Winwood posed his ill-advised question about whether the band could play. Rodgers replied that they were 'the best fuckin blues band in the world' and Fraser added that unless they realised that, they weren't signing. Here was that 'force' Blackwell subsequently referred to. Glover was astonished. 'Here they were, this bunch of nobodies that we'd advised Blackwell to pass on, a group of kids, laying down the law to Island.' Glover hadn't seen the half of it!

Blackwell: 'After I'd first seen the band I met with Guy Stevens who was somewhat of a genius in my opinion and Guy had this name for a band that he wanted to use and it seemed appropriate. So at the meeting I told them I thought we had a better name for them than Free. Andy asked me what it was and Guy said, "The Heavy Metal Kids". Andy, this kid of fourteen or something [actually sixteen], turned to me and calmly said, "Listen. If you want to sign us our name is Free."'

The Heavy Metal Kids! Can you imagine? We were appalled and said, 'It's Free or nothing.' They said it was The Heavy Metal Kids or nothing and so we left. We went back to my mum's house and wrote out the two names on two pieces of paper and put them both on the mantelpiece, looked at them and were even more certain. So, as the leader, it was my job to phone up Blackwell, just to keep open the contact, but still adamant that we weren't changing the name and he did his little cough and said, 'Well, it's the Heavy Metal Kids or we're not interested,' and I said, 'OK,' and slammed the phone down. All the others were looking at me. It was a very tense moment. As things stood, we'd turned them down. About five minutes later he called back and said, 'OK, you win.'

Free – and not The Heavy Metal Kids - had just secured a record deal.

ALL RIGHT NOW

A *madman greeted Andy and the band as they entered Island's Morgan studios in October '68 to begin recording their first LP. His name was Guy Stevens, great cascades of fuzzy hair down to his shoulders but completely receded on his forehead, sheepskin coat, rainbow scarf. He was Island's creative director, a huge music fan and already a convert to Free. The Heavy Metal Kids name they'd shrugged off had been his invention, just one of a torrent of madcap ideas that would issue from his lips or be noted down in his little book for some later use, possibly. He would be their producer, though his definition of producing was somewhat unconventional and was more to do with creating a conducive atmosphere – which might involve throwing chairs around or bouncing off the walls – than actually pressing any buttons. 'There are only two Phil Spectors, baby,' he once told the band Mott the Hoople, in reference to the legendary American producer, 'and I'm one of them!' Beneath the showbiz wacko was actually a sensitive soul who cared passionately about it all, who would go home at night and work on his musicologist list, trying to nail the crazy waves of connections fizzing in his head.*

It was only later I realised he was a speed freak and with hindsight that explains everything but it never entered my mind at the time – I thought that was just how he was, the Mad Hatter. His approach to producing was, 'Go play in the studio and see what comes out.' He was completely wild. It was all a little disorienting at first as we'd been put in the studio at the earliest possible opportunity and were very inexperienced in that environment.

Imagine the scene: the spliffed-out band, laid back almost horizontal amid a haze of hash smoke, then the mad, speed-fuelled producer talking at a million miles per hour, ideas spilling out of him, Andy and the boys somewhat nonplussed, wondering how you went about recording an album. Quite funny. A clash of drugs rather than personalities.

He coughed up ideas like hairballs, some were great, some less so. He had some bizarre idea of getting us to do this obscure Bob Dylan song for our first single, but I could never see how to do it and we didn't even rehearse it. Despite his wildness, he was actually quite influential with Blackwell. A lot of Blackwell's talent is putting people together and seeing what comes out and I detect his hand in putting us with Guy. Chris is such a very, very smart guy, with an extremely rare calibre of intelligence. Here he was, riding herd on the most extreme bunch of personalities, getting them to intermingle and create and making it all work, like some crazy quilt made up of human characters.

We also had Andy Johns, a sound engineer with a good sense of production and we really enjoyed working with him. But Guy wouldn't even know where the volume control was on the board! Because Free was such a live band it took a while to get used to the studio, the sound through the headphones and the fact there was no audience. There's no more sterile environment than a studio and it really takes you a while getting your head together. You do start to need to learn production and substitute the atmosphere an audience gives with double-tracking to fill out the sound. We were sort of agonising about what to do and eventually it was Guy who said, 'Just do your live set and we'll record it,' and that's pretty much what we did for that first album.

It was also Stevens who came up with the record's title, Tons Of Sobs, *just one of a torrent of his brilliant non-sequiturs and in this case working quite effectively in suggesting the band's blues credentials. This was from the man who'd come up with the name for the band Procol Harum (a mishearing of the pedigree name of a friend's cat) and later Mott the Hoople (from a character in a book he was reading while doing time in prison for drugs offences) and who would coin the title for The Rolling Stones' 1971 album* Sticky Fingers. *He'd been recruited by Blackwell years earlier to run his* blues/R&B label, Sue Records UK, and was a stalwart of the London music scene of the time, with regular DJ-ing gigs. Though he was a profound experimentalist, his first love was blues, hence his enthusiasm for this band of kids who were using that genre as a foundation but taking it in a new direction.

The 'British blues explosion' that Alexis Korner had helped create had quickly used up its credibility. Callow Brits singing about levees breaking and picking cotton just didn't ring true no matter how accurate the delivery and even when the lyrics weren't as explicitly Mississippi as that, the straight copyist template of the music suggested it. But that brief phase did kick-start a new sub-genre, one that early experimentalists like Cream and Jimi Hendrix had plugged into. Heady though their improvisation of blues with new, looser song structures and avant-garde guitar was, the form was still flowering and Free were lending it fresh shoots.

Some of the songs on Tons Of Sobs , like 'Going Down Slow', were pure traditional blues numbers. There were plenty of people around in the British blues boom of the time doing that sort of thing but what marked the band out as different even in these first faltering steps were tracks like 'I'm A Mover' (one of just two of the album's tracks co-written by Andy) or 'Walk In My Shadow', blues-based but with a strutting energy and driving rhythm and which invariably brought the house down when played live. Today they may sound like just fine examples of a familiar heavy blues-rock style but in the late-60s, this was fresh territory, and there was the suggestion of further new directions to come. In the song 'Over The Green Hills' – which Guy Stevens spliced in two, making it the opener and closer of the album with appropriate fade-out and fade-in – there is the beautiful, haunting acoustic material that would later figure much more prominently in the band's repertoire.

Coincidentally, on another side of London at much the same time another new band, Led Zeppelin were recording their first album and moving into much the same musical territory. Zeppelin's creative force, Jimmy Page, had been around the musical block, was a few years older than the Free boys, had established himself as the leading session musician of the time and had performed in The Yardbirds. His was the vision around which Zeppelin was formed. Although the two bands recorded their debut albums in the same month, Free already had a big live reputation and the notoriously magpie-like Page was an open admirer of their work. Rodgers had even been on a Page short-list of potential singers for his new band.

I guess the public were ready for a Free/Zeppelin sort of thing. We were all influenced by each other. We'd all be listening to The Beatles, The Stones, Cream etc. and interpreting it our own way. At any given time there's a collective vibe in the air which we as a population create – a certain tone on TV, the records that are being played, what is hip clothes-wise, a certain attitude – and good artists are highly attuned to that and can assimilate it very easily. The Beatles had it for a while and I think one of the magical elements of Free was that we had it. This was the particular emerging vibe of that specific time.

We actually met Robert Plant pre-Zeppelin at a gig we were doing in a club in Birmingham. He was singing with Alexis and he must've introduced himself to us in such a way that we took to him because we all ended up back at our hotel room jamming, singing Beatles and soul songs. He was telling us that he'd been invited to join this new group and he didn't know whether to take a flat wage from it or be on a percentage. We advised him strongly he should be on a percentage. His voice that night in the hotel room sounded better than I've ever heard it since, incidentally. It was a fun night. But when Zeppelin's first album came out and they had part of 'The Hunter' – which was an Albert King song but a big number in our live set – in there it did strike me as a little odd.

What we'd been performing live up to this point was pretty much what was on that first record. So I hadn't really started to develop fully with my songwriting. In songwriting terms there was more Paul and less me than on subsequent records, just because Paul was at that stage further down the road with that side of things. It was a pretty good starting point for a first album, I think, but only once we'd got that down did we have time to reflect on how it could have been and where we wanted to go next. *Tons Of Sobs* was pretty much the arrangement I think Koss was envisaging, with a straight interplay between the singer and guitarist, sort of like how Rod Stewart and Jeff Beck had been together – the powerful singer interspersed with the great solo blues guitarist. But as Paul and I began to develop our songwriting together, it moved away from that, new horizons opened up and that was maybe the beginning of some difficulty for Koss. It was a surprise change of direction for him and not one he really knew how to deal with. He liked it but had trouble keeping up with it, presenting quite a conundrum for him.

Paul R had ended up staying with me at my mum's house for a few weeks while he made other living arrangements and during this time we did a lot of writing together. In fact most of the second album was written during that time. Koss had moved out from his parents' house to a girlfriend's flat in Covent Garden. I'd been around to his family's place only once. His father was quite a famous actor and so they had money and it was a pretty nice house in Golders Green. Koss was the only one of the four of us from an affluent background, but he had a rebellious relationship with his father. We were in Koss's room jamming when his dad appeared and said, very sternly, 'Paul. A word,' and walked out – and I thought, 'Fuck, I don't like this guy.' The fact that Koss had gone from his classical guitar to a rock group was just part of his rebellion, but it was a quiet sort of rebellion, a sort of 'I'm not going to go the way you want me to' attitude, but they still talked. On one of Koss's later solo albums there was a picture of him standing with his guitar plugged into a trash can and the name Kossoff above it, just slinging more mud in his father's face.

Tons Of Sobs *received good reviews but sold only around 20,000 copies – not enough to get it into the album charts. However, the band's live following was building momentum region by region, the venues getting steadily bigger. They now had a new Transit van courtesy of Island, they had a hash budget, a full-time roadie in Graham Whyte, the fit of their clothes was improving – and Andy was now in charge of an ever-increasing flow of gig income. He'd turn up at the Island offices with a big bag of money and a summary of incomings and outgoings, then be off again, leaving the staff there somewhat bemused. This sixteen-year-old looked like a rock star, played like a rock star, smoked hash like a rock star – but he did the books!*

At first I was so pernickety I'd go into the Island offices with their fifteen per cent in pennies and other change, all of it accounted for down to the last penny. After a while they sort of laughed and said they could wait until it got bigger. So then I'd usually deposit it in a bank local to my mother's home, we'd pay ourselves a weekly wage – about £50 at first – allow for expenses and the spliffs of Red Lebanese hash that we were so partial to. Sometimes Island's booking agency would receive advances for certain appearances on our behalf and so once a month I'd sit down with their accountant and reconcile who had received what and make adjustments to keep everything square – which it always was. There was never any question of one side feeling the other was pulling a fast one; Island just wasn't like that.

The first region to be truly conquered by Free was the north-east of England, and Sunderland in particular. Geoff Docherty was a doorman who had branched out into concert promotion for the Bay Hotel in Seaburn, the seaside part of Sunderland. The Bay had a ballroom that could accommodate around 500 and Free were Docherty's second ever booking there, on January 13, 1969, at a fee of £35. At the next appearance there, in June, they played two sets to a much bigger crowd – and created a sensation, according to this account of Docherty's from his book A Rock Promoter's Tale: *'The Bay never knew what had hit it... Rodgers commanded the stage as if he was a young Elvis Presley... Kossoff, his dextrous fingers bent and sustained the notes with the intensity of a heart surgeon straining to save an endangered life. There was a majestic subtlety about his playing as the notes climbed and soared...Andy Fraser seemed to take it all in his stride, outwardly cool and unruffled... Simon Kirke hitting the drums with sledgehammer precision... When they eventually left the stage to a tumultuous roar of appreciation, they were drenched in sweat and drained of every last ounce of energy. Overnight Free had become our superstars. The rest of the country weren't to latch onto them for several months.'*

Actually, there was still some energy left post-gig, as Docherty recalls, 'female admirers waiting to meet their new young heroes in Free, especially Paul Rodgers. I'd never experienced female adulation of this intensity and found it impossible to empty The Bay that night. After checking with the group, I let a number of girls into their dressing room... Girls were flinging their arms around them in an unbridled show of affection. After coming off stage they had looked exhausted in the summer heat, but it soon became apparent they were eager to capitalise on their extremely good fortune... When the group left The Bay hordes of girls followed them out. I don't know how many ended up in the group's van, but there were a good few vacant seats on the late buses.'

Free were now way too big for The Bay and for their next Sunderland appearance Docherty booked the Locarno (ironically nicknamed the Fillmore North in homage to the American venues Fillmore East and West), a 3,000-seater venue. Docherty: 'As evening approached I drove over the town bridge and was astonished to see hundreds of people making their way towards The Fillmore on foot. As I pulled up there was already a huge queue snaking hundreds of yards away from the main entrance and within an hour the gig was packed to capacity, with hundreds locked out. Were Free going to be bigger than The Beatles? It seems a silly question now, but that night, far from being silly, it looked like a realistic possibility. Halfway through the set they announced 'The Hunter'. The hall erupted into a frenzy and more girls pretended to faint in a vain attempt to be lifted onto the stage. When the band finally came off stage, I walked out into the ballroom still in a daze. "When are they coming back?" was a question I must've been asked a thousand times... Such was their unifying power even the bouncers liked this group.'

If their performance that night was sensational, their fee was pretty impressive too – for 1969. Just eight months after appearing for £35, they were now commanding £1,500 – and Docherty's negotiations were invariably through Andy. As a point of comparison, Docherty was able to secure The Who for £500 at around the same time for the same venue, Eric Clapton's Derek and the Dominoes a year later for £750. Yet other parts of the country had still barely heard of Free. Once experienced though, they were not forgotten.

We could be pretty awesome live. Koss was invariably at the centre of this, the one that hit you first, just an incredible performer, visually and sonically very,

very exciting. As far as Free live were concerned he *was* the band – that was the perception. But we went to a lot of care to ensure that we came on ready for maximum attack right from the off. We would get there together hours before the gig to set up and rehearse. Then we would always have a practice amp with us in the dressing room and we'd play in there before going on. I think all bands should do it and I'm amazed they don't. We would get a really good groove going and then just take that with us onto the stage. We were already flying by the time we got out there. In the early days we didn't always have a big crowd to perform for – but then we'd just perform for ourselves and still have a great time. In fact one of the very best gigs we ever played was in front of about twelve people at some place in Wales when we were just astounding, though I do say so myself. Another extraordinary thing about it was during the break between the two sets one of the dozen punters said, 'I bet you £10 I can eat this beer mug.' We said, 'OK,' - and he did. There was no trick – he did; crunched the glass in his mouth and swallowed it all. We were impressed but not as much as we'd impressed ourselves with our playing that night. It was the best we ever played, and hardly anyone was there to witness it.

Britain continued to awaken to Free region by region even as Blackwell was putting together plans to tour them in the USA in support of Blind Faith. In the meantime, much of the material that Andy and Paul Rodgers had written together at Andy's mum's house - and which would later surface on the band's second album, Free, *in October – was being introduced into their live sets. It was a definite evolution from the material on* Tons Of Sobs, *all of it slow or mid-tempo, not as heavily blues-derived, much of it beautifully haunting. Here was that melancholic 'soldier boy' side of Rodgers that Andy was encouraging. It was a style of music that didn't sit comfortably with Kossoff.*

As we developed the type of music we were doing it required more guitar chord playing rather than plain blues guitar and I think it sort of left Koss going, 'What the fuck happened there?' Although he'd had this classical training he couldn't seem to link his acoustic and blues playing, it was like they were two different worlds for him and he really struggled with chords, never really made the connection. Sometimes when I'd present a song that didn't have those usual three chords and say, 'No, just play the blues guitar while these chords are going on around you,' it would throw him. He'd get kind of panicky, he'd hear these different chords in the song and feel he had to play a different sort of solo and that wasn't the case at all. He was being required to do stuff he never thought he'd be asked to do. He really thought, 'Oh this is my band, this is what we're going to do,' and then I come along and say, 'No, we're going this way,' so I think it was definitely hardest on him. And I think whereas he thought there was going to be a guitar/singer type of relationship like a Jeff Beck/Rod Stewart thing, there ended up being a Paul/Andy writing thing which he had to really run to keep up with so it did make it very difficult for him. I've since often wondered whether if we'd had a rhythm guitarist it might have made a difference, by freeing Koss up a bit.

Often, it would be Fraser's bass doing the job of rhythm guitar, every bit as much a key part of the band's unique sound as Kossoff's wailing lead. This ambiguity of the guitarist's role may have been a contributory factor to what both Simon Kirke and Chris Blackwell recall as a brief split in the band, but of which Andy has no concrete memory. Kirke reckons that the choice of the band's first single was the first hint of two conflicting schools of musical thought in the band. The Fraser/Rodgers song 'Broad Daylight' – borrowed from the forthcoming second album – was slow-paced and downbeat but with an uplift in the melody that reflected its optimistic lyrics. It did not sell well. 'It was a disaster,' says Kirke. 'I think it sold three copies in Sheffield! Andy was really insistent it become the single but both Koss and I felt it didn't really represent the band's sound as we were both still blues men at heart. I think Andy had more pure talent than any of us and he's a fantastic musician, someone I'd work with again in a heartbeat, but our differing views on that single represented where we were at at that time. With hindsight, Paul and Andy had a more progressive vision than us.' It was a conflict that apparently escalated, Kirke and others recalling that Andy and Paul Rodgers planned to go it alone and that, under the supervision of Guy Stevens, recruitment for their replacements got underway in order for Free to continue with Kossoff and Kirke. They even got as far as auditioning bass player Pete Watts, who later joined Island's Mott the Hoople. 'Andy and Paul Rodgers came to see me at my home in London that I worked out of,' says Blackwell, 'and told me they wanted to split from the other two. I was horrified and very against it.'

It only half rings a bell. I didn't realise things had gone that far from their point of view but I do recall a bit of a rift. I think there was maybe a feeling from Paul R and myself, once we really got going with the songwriting, we were going in a new direction and we were like, 'OK, guys, are you coming along or what?' and that maybe we felt they were a bit slow to follow that. I don't recall it as all that serious but I guess it was if they were auditioning.

However serious the rift, it was quickly over and by the middle of June '69 the four were hard at work in the studio putting together that second album. Blackwell took over production duties himself on this record, perhaps recognising that the chaotic creative tension of Guy Stevens wouldn't have been appropriate to the moment. The album Free *had much the same intimate 'there in the room' production feel as their debut, the same pared-down arrangements, but the songs were slower paced, often deeply mournful, more acoustic, more sophisticated than before but with the band's latent power growling away, as if waiting to be given its head, lending the album a delicious tension. It's a beautiful piece of work, a collection of nine songs that seep gently but deeply into you. Eight of them are credited to the Fraser/Rodgers songwriting partnership and it's apparent with the distance of hindsight that they were pushing new boundaries at a stage when Kossoff and Kirke were still caught up in the idea of being in a 'blues-rock' band. It might even be that the tension this created was what lent the music that very quality. Certainly the intensity of this group of people was profound, as related by Johnny Glover, who after that first unpromising meeting with the band had quickly grown to love them: 'I went to their first or second show and when you saw them with an audience they were so exciting. I went back to the office and said, "They're fantastic." I'd fallen in love with them and I realised that Blackwell had been right to ignore our earlier opinions. They remain the greatest band I have ever seen. But the energy and aggression they had on stage came at a price. The way they built themselves up to do a show was almost like a football team or something so when they came on they were totally focussed. When they came off it took a while for that to drain away. I've never experienced it with any other band. I've seen bands be committed and serious, but this was way beyond that. It was safer just to leave them, let them come down, stay out until someone came out the door, sometimes the roadie who'd say, "Yeah, it's OK now." I've never known a band like it. They would get tied up to an incredible degree if anything had gone the slightest bit wrong. The intensity of them was unreal.'*

I wouldn't say that was inaccurate, but it's Johnny's perspective. It didn't necessarily feel as volatile as that inside. We sure were intense, but as a unit could handle each other. As an 'outsider' Johnny may have been wise to stay away. And if there was stuff to work out between us, there was nothing an outsider could do, but get hit. We did have a mellowness, but maybe just after a gig wasn't the best time to see it on display!

In fact if anything, I would say we didn't voice differences of opinion enough – most of it was just vibe. Certainly, I don't recall Koss ever voicing his frustrations about the musical direction we were going in, but in hindsight I'm sure they were there. I guess me showing him the finger positions for chords was demeaning for him, but I was only ever trying for what was the appropriate sound.

The album kicks off with 'I'll Be Creeping', a mid-pace number with a sinister sound to match its message, based around the repeated, very deliberate, mid-paced guitar line that introduces the song. There's a raging solo from Koss and a sweet, soft middle refrain that contrasts powerfully with the menace of the rest of it. The song was initiated by Andy.

It's all based on that simple riff. I started that and 'Woman' on the same day. Paul R put the lyrics to 'I'll Be Creeping' and I still think they're great – the idea of the spurned lover creeping around looking to take his revenge. Blackwell had us release it as a single because it has quite an 'up' groove but I was always resistant to the idea; I didn't think it had enough of a chorus to make a single and it didn't sell that well. That said, Blackwell did have a very good ear. He was quite capable of walking into a playback and saying, 'That needs some tambourine there,' and he was usually right.

'Songs of Yesterday' was the album's second track and introduced a heavily bass-led funky element into the band's repertoire for the first time, repeating the trick on the fourth number 'Trouble On Double Time'. Rodgers' voice on these is particularly fabulous, projecting the songs, lending Andy's driving motion formidable power, the uncluttered sound amplifying the impact of Kossoff's tasteful flourishes. In between these songs nestles the supremely laid-back 'Lying In The Sunshine', the hash-mellow soul of the band laid languidly bare. For Fraser's current tastes it's a little too mellow:

There was a lot of hash involved with that one! Way too much. At the time that mellowness seemed really appropriate but when I hear it now, no, it needs an up. It would lend itself very well to a reggae treatment, like a lot of Free songs actually.

The supine vibe continues with the instrumental 'Mouthful Of Grass', then it's onto the power-house resigned lament of 'Woman'. 'Free Me' and 'Mourning Sad Morning' – separated in the running order by the divisive 'Broad Daylight' – are melancholy, beautiful and might even be classified as folk music. The latter song features a flute solo from a guesting Chris Wood, formerly a member of the Island-based Traffic, a band that had temporarily broken up at this time following Steve Winwood's defection to the short-lived Blind Faith.

Chris Wood was a bit of an odd one. Once Traffic had split he didn't know what to do with himself and since we'd brought him in to provide flute on 'Mourning Sad Morning' he'd just sort of continued hanging round with us, me in particular. He was another one that ended up sleeping on my mother's couch for a couple of months and I didn't really know what his plans were, so at some point I said, 'OK, Chris, we're off to the States next week,' and he said, 'Oh, I'm coming too.' OK... He was absolutely terrified of flying and had to get himself juiced out of his mind just to get on the plane but he made the flight with us. Then he came to the hotel with us, then slept on my floor and continued doing so for the next few weeks. None of us had any idea what was going on with him but we just sort of let it drift on; it was the weirdest thing.

Wisely, Island had booked us into a New York club called Ungano's for a week to warm us up before going to the big venues with Blind Faith and we also played there in between the Blind Faith gigs. We were opening there for Doctor John and The Night Trippers. Chris fell for one of Doctor John's backing singers, there was a lot of smack around at the time, the pair of them became smack-heads and he left our orbit. He was a nice guy but kind of unfocussed, I never did really get him. Sadly he died some years later of causes connected to his various addictions.

Thinking back, I'm actually quite surprised he was clean of drugs when we came through customs on first arriving in America – because we were all given a very hard time by the customs people. Long hair on a man was still very much disapproved of in America and they just sort of automatically assumed you were a junkie. The customs people interviewed us very aggressively, went through all our things, even our toothpaste tubes. I was just waiting for them to put on the rubber gloves. Thankfully they didn't because at that point I think I would have just turned around and gone back home!

We'd made sure none of us were carrying any traces of hash and I don't think even Koss at that time was on anything heavier than that. He may have been getting into the mandrax at that stage but I don't think so – there was no outward sign of it. He was still very up and funny, just as he'd always been.

Actually we found hash was quite difficult to get hold of in the States at that time and we were smoking grass instead and it took me quite a few weeks before I realised that actually I didn't like it. It gave me a feeling of paranoia and none of that nice chilled-out feeling you get from hash.

We were as impressed as anyone ever is on their first visit to the States – the hugeness of everything, the buildings, the cars. We saw the other side too and although the civil rights fight had already been won by then you could see it was still no paradise for blacks. There was an aggression about the place that I was unaccustomed to. I was walking in New York City one time and stopped to ask two cops for directions – a very British thing to do in hindsight – and maybe because of my accent they thought I was taking the piss. One of them raised his boot as though to kick, a sort of 'get outa here, kid' gesture and that did take me aback. It was at the time of the Moon landings and I recall watching some fuzzy TV pictures of that in some motel somewhere. Actually, it didn't strike me as such a big deal at the time – I thought it was inevitable that the future had arrived and there'd be lots more stuff like that.

We were playing at Ungano's one night and were surprised to see Eric Clapton and Ginger Baker from Blind Faith in the audience. We hadn't really had much contact with them before then, so it was quite a big deal that they'd come to see us play. It was an even bigger deal for Koss when Clapton asked him afterwards to show him how he got that great vibrato sound from the guitar. Clapton was one of Koss's idols so this was a massive deal to him. He was like, 'What? You want *me* to show *you* !' He was walking on air for days afterwards.

Most of that tour is now just a blur for me. At the time, and for years to come, the memories were crystal clear. But in the painful part of letting go of what had turned from a dream to a nightmare, details have been lost. I do remember though that Blind Faith wanted to drive down the magnificent Pacific coast Highway One from San Francisco to LA and drink in the scenic route and so both bands and managers etc. shared a coach and on one occasion we climbed into it and there was a totem pole running the full length of the floor we had to clamber over. Apparently Clapton had seen it and decided he just had to buy it to take home.

I remember a gig at the Winterland in San Francisco we did without Blind Faith and that I was really looking forward to because it was being promoted by Billy Graham. I was expecting a really cool vibe but instead it was a really shitty vibe, with the roadies complaining like hell about the way they were being treated. The audience were pretty cool though, as they were for most of our gigs.

The American experience had been chaotic, the tour under-prepared, partly a function of the low budget Island allocated for a band that had not yet taken off commercially. The Madison Square Gardens debacle was an unfortunate introduction but they bounced back from it, even got standing ovations at other venues from crowds that had come to see the headline act, not them. It gave them yet more depth of experience and their camaraderie saw them through the worst of it. It also led to them forming a bond with Johnny Glover, as he recalls: 'I guess I became an honorary member on the American tour in '69 at Boston. We were all staying at a motel – the budget was really tight. The ice was broken when one of them said, "We need to sort out your image – Andy's going to give you a haircut." And he gave me a crew cut.

'But even though we bonded, I was never "inside" the band – no-one was, only them. They had this incredible independence, power and assurance. It was as if Island worked for them, not the other way around!' Shortly after their return to the UK – by way of a brief appearance at the Isle of Wight Festival they would rule the following year – the album Free was released. It reached number 22 in the UK album charts, nothing startling for such a wonderful piece of work, and paling into insignificance alongside the success juggernaut of their contemporaries Led Zeppelin, but it was at least building solid foundations.

Actually, the two bands might have been label mates, as Glover explains: 'We almost signed Zeppelin. [Zeppelin's manager] Peter Grant – whose office was in the floor above ours in Oxford Street – brought the completed first album to us and we offered more money than we'd offered anyone, a fortune, but Atlantic offered more and Chris said, "Sorry, Peter, but I can't match that,' and Atlantic made sure they put everything behind Zep – to recoup their investment. Peter Grant was the one that changed the record business, made it a much bigger business. Up to then it had all been a bit toy-town. Peter had the promoters take a percentage of the gate. Before that, bands had been paid a flat fee. He was an aggressive visionary and the essential difference, I would say, in the differing levels of success between Free and Zeppelin.'

Grant was a bombastic, terrifyingly aggressive hustler and veteran of the music business. He hyped his boys massively before anyone had even heard a note of their music, built them up into something massive and secured a huge deal with Atlantic Records, catapulting them instantly into the fast lane in terms of promotional budget and attention. But there was something else too: Zeppelin's members were that crucial few years older than the Free guys. As a unit they were tougher and, as such, ready for the instant hyper-success. They would go on to become the biggest band of the 1970s by quite some margin, leaving Free as a fond, short-lived memory.

Blackwell accepts that the vast difference in resources between Island and Atlantic might account for the respective levels of commercial success of Free and Zeppelin, but isn't sure Free would have been ready. 'I always believed in a steady build-up,' he says, 'as success too quickly is very hard to sustain and the boys were very young. Zeppelin were well into their mid-to-late twenties.'

Hardier, more resilient, bigger and longer-lived, Zeppelin weren't idealists like Free; rather they were chancers, looking for the main chance and recognising it when it came. There was a musical vision behind them – Jimmy Page's – but it was shared by the others only through the necessities of the moment and it wasn't as organic or inclusive as Free's. Zep were older, not necessarily wiser, but had been around the block enough to toughen up, just like The Stones had before them. They could bend in *the wind more than Free. But they weren't better.*

I guess the bottom line is that Zeppelin stayed around and didn't fall apart. Peter Grant worked on the principle of intimidation – to promoters and record companies and anyone in the way. He was prepared to break body parts to get what he wanted for his band. Later Paul Rodgers would become seduced by that approach but I wanted nothing to do with it. That all came much later though. In these early years we didn't particularly measure ourselves against the success of Zeppelin even though we did look with some puzzlement at how huge they'd become. We weren't particular fans of their music, thought they were a bit heavy-handed actually. They took very heavily from the old blues people whereas I don't feel we did. They also took from Free and turned the whole thing into a very successful commodity. They are quite open about our influence on them. We were quite satisfied with the way we were building up our following and were totally sure we were on-course, that it was all going to come. Chris Blackwell wasn't aggressive at all, just very smart, very sympathetic and much more suited to our personalities than someone like Peter Grant would have been. We felt we controlled our own destiny and were happy with how we were growing. It was a very different dynamic to Zeppelin, I think.

Free's breakthrough to major success was by now just around the corner, however, and it came from the sound of weak applause that had died even before they left the stage one rainy night – probably at a Durham university gig, early November 1969.

Simon says it was Durham but I have no firm memories of exactly where it was that 'All Right Now' was first sparked. All I remember was that it was a rainy Tuesday or something in some god-forsaken college. We got lost finding our way there so we were in a foul mood to begin with. We didn't get enough time to get our groove going beforehand, there weren't enough people and they were all shit-faced on mandrax, all kind of bumping into each other like the rubber people. Usually that wouldn't have bothered us. We played plenty of places where we just played for ourselves and had a great time. But this night, we were just in a foul mood and we didn't play that well because of it.

We came off and were pretty pissed off with ourselves and each other and there was a lot of sadness in the dressing room. You could've heard a pin drop, it was very uncomfortable. It just needed something to sort of break the silence and the bad vibe and I just started riffing 'All Right Now', like a parent soothing a kid: 'It's OK. We'll live tomorrow and it'll be fine.' Basically that was how the chorus came. Later I came up with the guitar riff at the beginning – I was trying for something with the power of The Who. The chorus guitar riff was originally on piano and we translated it for guitar which was no easy feat. It's very easy on a piano but they don't always translate well. The bass part was just trying to find something that was enough support and which suggested chords while Koss was playing a solo. That's all there was to it. The verses Paul wrote, they were just kind of knock-off teenage fantasy. I don't think he paid them too much attention, they were just appropriate. We kinda liked it because it was an up-tempo song. Before that, we didn't really have any up-tempo songs in the set but I think we were so stoned we didn't realise that! The mid-tempo ones we thought were up-tempo!

Andy gives a characteristic amused 'mmm' at this, his eyes sparkling a path through the decades so you can see the seventeen-year-old him within the fifty-six-year-old face. Not that he looks like most fifty-six-year-olds; he still looks like a rock star, hip clothes, trim figure, super-fit looking thanks to those endless hours working out each morning and a food intake that is carefully monitored and bolstered as part of his health regime. No drugs other than medicinal ones, an occasional glass of wine with his evening meal. His illness has forced him into an even stricter discipline than the one he already possessed. The ravages of that illness can be glimpsed sometimes, a slight hollowness of the face in a certain light – but it's nothing compared to how he looked when his doctors were climbing the walls wondering what to try next. He was fortunate in the timing of the drug and treatment advances. They came along just in time for him. He was fortunate too that he could pay for cutting edge treatment and drugs. The basis of that fortune is 'All Right Now', one of the very few songs to have been awarded the '3 million plus' honour by the BMI (Broadcast Music Inc.), this a reference to how many times it has been played on American radio. Someone has worked out that even today it is being played on radio somewhere in the world an average of once every 45 seconds. It has sold well in excess of five million copies.

It's a seminal rock anthem, simple, strutting, sing-along, happy, boy-meets-girl celebratory. It sounds like the smell of summer. The four-syllable guitar intro that defines the shape of the verses gives it a straightforward power, but those chords that are played with such pin-point precision by Kossoff didn't come easy to the guitarist. 'He made it sound magic,' says Andy, 'but it was very difficult for him. Again I had to physically show him.' The jerky groove of the verses is so irresistible it needs no help from the bass – which doesn't come in until the chorus.

Actually the way the single sounded was down to Chris Blackwell, who was really overseeing that whole third album. The album track 'All Right Now' was longer and had a Koss solo in it and Blackwell told us we needed to lose a verse and the solo for the single. This was on top of quite a few other things he had changed about the production of the album from what we had first done and it got quite heavy between us and him for a while. But he got his way and he turned out to be right. We recorded most of the album at Trident House, using a house engineer there called Roy Thomas Baker. But then Blackwell wanted us to finish it at Island's own new studios – and we had to sneak Roy out there in the middle of the night, panic-stricken, sweating, terrified of Trident finding out he was working for someone else. He didn't want his name on the album for that reason. You under-estimated Blackwell at your peril; you might have thought, 'What does he know about the music?' but actually he could translate what was happening right now into sound. He was the guy that would later take Bob Marley and convince him that he needed to incorporate some rock into his reggae sound – and knew which players to bring in to accomplish that – thereby making him a huge star. He was very highly attuned to what the audience was ready to receive and his feeling about 'All Right Now' – which he told us as soon as he heard it was going to be a smash hit – turned out to be spot-on.

'All Right Now' was recorded in January 1970 and released as a single in May in both the UK and the USA. It was one of seven songs that would feature on the Fire & Water *album that followed in the single's wake. The single entered the UK charts at number four and peaked at number two (held off the top spot by Mungo Jerry's 'In The Summertime'). The suspicion is that Island, caught unaware by demand in excess of one thousand copies per hour, had not pressed enough records and couldn't deliver in time, thereby preventing it from hitting the top spot. It stayed in the top 10 for almost three months. In terms of total numbers sold, as opposed to its peak in any one week, it comfortably out-sold 'In The Summertime'. In the US, it made number four.* Fire & Water *reached number two in the UK albums chart, number seventeen in America and would go on to sell over a million copies. This was a different scale of success to anything the band had experienced before. Free had cracked the big time. They duly made their appearance on the British TV institution,* Top of the Pops, *forced to mime along to their own record for the sake of the cameras, Andy blatantly not playing his instrument in one of the most uncommitted mimes of all time.*

The shit hit the fan with the success of that song but for a while it was all still good – because we were still a unit able to laugh at the craziness of it all. That song brought a whole different type of fan, teenage girls especially, and even though we'd experienced big crowds before at venues where we were popular, this was a different sort of craziness – unearthly. You'd get out the car near a gig and people were trying to tear lumps out of you, trying to get some of your hair as a souvenir, as if you were not a human being but just some 3D version of the picture they'd seen in a magazine. They are not responding to you as a human, someone who might feel pain. I was really offended by that, it was very dehumanising and it gave me just a slight idea of what it must've been like for The Beatles. That stuff sent all sorts of alarm bells ringing for me, created quite a profound reaction in me. If this was what fame was like, be very, very careful. When it's the four of you inside the car all banded together you can deal with it, laugh at it, make private jokes with each other about it – 'This is absurd and we all know it is.' But as soon as that camaraderie isn't there anymore and you still have to deal with that shit – that's a very lonely place to be. That's one of the things on the long list of what breaks bands up.

In time there came to be some resentment from within the band and from Free's more purist fans about 'All Right Now'. Kossoff, the biggest blues purist of them all, was quite vocal in dismissing the song in interviews as 'frivolous' and not representing what the band were about. But realistically, as well as being a great pop song that still retained the band's powerhouse sound, it also brought attention to them, got people to investigate further, maybe encouraged them to buy the album – which was another fabulously potent collection of songs, arguably the band at the very height of its powers. It was a further evolution in their sound in that many of the songs could easily have been soul covers with a different arrangement. Paul Rodgers was trying for a Wilson Pickett vibe with the title song 'Fire & Water' – and he evidently got it spot on because a few months later Pickett himself recorded it; brass section in place of guitar, it sounded just as good.

Our influences were getting broader. At that time we had The Band on the car's tape player a lot and also Joni Mitchell but then we began getting into more R&B stuff like Isaac Hayes. Koss turned us all onto Gladys Knight and The Staple Singers. 'Fire & Water' was started off by Paul; he had the melody and the lyrics and I just worked out the musical arrangement. Interestingly Simon – who was as opposed to drum solos as I was to bass solos – resisted the idea of the little drum solo at the end but when he did it, it was a killer.

After the slowed-down power-funk of the title track came one of those beautiful haunting Free ballads, 'Oh I Wept', a gently strummed minor chord sequence segueing into a wistful Paul Rodgers moan to get it underway, the restrained drums and deep bass not coming in until almost half a minute into the song. Kossoff's guitar is at its most emotive even though it's being held in check, there's a mid-tempo middle section with lyrics that put you right there – 'I take my seat upon the train, and let the sun come melt my pain. Come tomorrow I'll be far away. In the sunshine of another day' – before it reverts back. It was a relatively rare songwriting contribution from Kossoff.

Koss just came into the studio with that lovely sequence of chords already worked out and it didn't take much to get it down. It's got a lovely vibe and gives a good insight into Koss's character, I think. I can feel him even now when I hear the melody of that middle section. The song 'Remember' was a reworking of something we had left over from the first album and it was started by me, quite a boppy groove in the version on the record and which I now think would lend itself brilliantly well to reggae. We all liked it and actually thought it should have been our single, not 'All Right Now'! But Blackwell was adamant. We had quite a few arguments with him about that. Shows how much we knew! As a song it's more substantial than 'All Right Now', there's more truth in the lyrics as opposed to the total fantasy fairy tale of 'All Right Now'. But Blackwell knew what he was doing.

'Heavy Load' is a classic Free plaintive account of a man on a difficult journey. It's piano-led, with gorgeous minor keys lending the song the desired tone, and was constructed by Andy on that faithful old out-of-tune pub piano bought him by his mum all those years ago.

I still like that song, I like the sense of the lyrics and the movement. It has a real sense of maturity, and from the vantage point of today I'm sometimes quite taken aback at how remarkably mature we were for teenagers. I was seventeen when we recorded this and none of us were yet out of our teens.

'Mr Big' is a big, menacing, powerful brute of a song introduced and sustained by a simple three-note motif and features Andy performing one of the most remarkable pieces of extended bass playing in recorded history.

We were in my bedroom at my mum's house, Simon had the bass in his hands and just happened to hit those three key notes. I immediately stopped him and said, 'Do that again, Simon, I like that,' and the song was written from there. Even at this stage we were still jamming at mum's house. I was still living there, the two Pauls were living with their respective girlfriends. Paul R and Simon had flats in the same building in Holborn and we'd sometimes go there, but more often than not it was in Roehampton. The bass 'solo' – though it's not really a solo because the other instruments are still playing – was my attempt at the sort of thing I used to hear Binky McKenzie play and came to mind after I heard an Isaac Hayes song in which the bass just launched into this wild, abandoned extended piece.

FOUR MEN ON AN ISLAND

Before 'All Right Now' signs the album off, there's a pretty, pretty ballad, 'Don't Say You Love Me', where the heartbroken voice of the song implores his woman not to tell him she loves him 'because I know it would be just a lie'.

I have no clear memory of how that one came together though I think Simon had something to do with its inception. The lyrics are definitely Paul's. It's a pretty good song and listening to it now I'm struck by Simon's drumming. He really does have a unique approach. Even though he loves a lot of black music, he plays like a white drummer, always on the one, really leaning on it like a metronome whereas most black drummers are on the two, putting the dance into it.

Free were on top of the world and confirmation of their status came with their appearance at 1970's Isle of Wight Festival in August. With 'All Right Now' one of the defining sounds of that summer, they got a pretty ecstatic reaction from a crowd estimated at somewhere between 400,000 and 600,000. Certainly in the region of half a million people were camped out on the hillside to hear Bob Dylan, Jimi Hendrix, Joni Mitchell, The Who, Free and many others. It was the British answer to Woodstock, the original outdoor rock festival. Free had played a limited set here the year before, immediately after their American tour, but their place near the end of the bill combined with the over-running of the acts before them meant they got just fifteen minutes. Their status one year on meant that was never going to happen, with Chris Blackwell very active behind the scenes to ensure a good slot for his boys, probably pushing against an open door such was the popularity of that single crowd-pleasing song.

Blackwell had gone to a lot of trouble to make sure it worked for us. We were due to go on one day at what would have been a bad time and he finagled it so we went on next day at a much better time and it really worked for us. He made sure things went smoothly, organised a helicopter to fly us in which was unheard of then, picked us up from our hotel on the island, dropped us off right behind the back-stage area. I remember from high in the air the pilot pointing out what looked like a tiny little square among a mass of people, telling us that was the stage. You can't imagine what trying to get in and out of those places is like; you'd be wiped out before you got there. If you're there for hours before going on you're drained by the energy of all the people. This way we were still fresh when we went on, which is really important. The energy from that amount of people just sucks it out of you. All that energy is directed at you and it can sort of melt you, that's the only way I can describe it. You looked out at the crowd from stage and literally they went as far as the horizon, a mind-blowing view. The whole thing felt a little other-worldly actually, right from the time we were on the ferry getting over there and The Who's Pete Townshend knocked on our car window and said, 'Great song, boys,' very graciously and in a very English accent very different to what I'd have expected. I'd assumed he'd talk like a London street kid but actually he sounded more like Prince Charles. Later, we caught The Who's set. They were a fantastic spectacle live, so dynamic, Townshend such a performer in his white painter's outfit, windmilling his arms, Roger Daltrey coming at you like a thug going berserk. I thought visually and dynamically they were better than us – but we had our own thing.

When we climbed out of the helicopter I was aware of what I can only describe as an alien vibe – and there was Tiny Tim, one of the performers, and just the weirdest individual I've ever encountered. When you tried to communicate with him he definitely wasn't of this planet, just a weird being. It all just added to the unreal buzz. It was a beautiful day, not too hot, not too cold, as a band we were still in great shape spiritually and physically, with years of touring behind us and a big hit. We were riding high. We met the energy and gave a good account of ourselves, I think.

We had everything going for us on that day. Even the sound system guy had a link with us in that he was a guy Paul and I used to make demos with round his house on a two-track which back then seemed very advanced. His brother was the festival promoter, Gary Farr. As this guy had since progressed to having his own PA company, his brother had given him the gig to do the festival's sounds. They made sure everything worked in our favour.

Having said that, it was only when I watched the DVD *Free Forever* that I was reminded that when we first went on Koss had a problem with a buzzing from his speaker and we had to stop for a minute or two while it was sorted. That sort of thing in front of half a million people gets your nerves quite jangly, but we recovered from it fine, we met the energy that was focussed upon us. But when we came off, even though we hadn't been on particularly long, we were absolutely exhausted – and I'm sure that was just from having all that energy from so many people focussed on us. We'd done much longer gigs than that before without using up anything like so much energy.

These momentous events are all explained in Andy's usual coolly laid-back tone, significant moments underlined by nothing more than a twinkling smile or an amused 'mmm'. You get the impression that he was exactly like that as these things were happening around him, measured, taking it all in, understanding the significance of everything but never overwhelmed by it, knowing the job he had to do, keeping everything on course, a keen intellect processing all that was coming at the four of them. That's certainly how it looks in the footage of the time, the quiet force in the eye of the storm – just turned eighteen years old standing on that Isle of Wight stage looking at the infinite horizon of dancing bodies; a young god with the world at his feet.

In the wake of the whole thing I'm pretty sure Blackwell must have had a hand in getting us on the front cover of *Time* for a feature they did on the festival itself. They used a picture of us to illustrate it even though there were bigger acts than us on such as Hendrix or Dylan.

Maybe, but Blackwell himself doesn't recall any involvement in that. More likely, the magazine's editors just felt that Free were more 'of the moment' than the longer-established acts – that and their extreme youth and how fantastic they looked. See a picture of Free performing and it instantly says 'circa 1970': the hair, the clothes, the mannerisms. They visually freeze-frame that moment. If you are old enough to have memories of that summer in Britain, chances are they are soaked in the sound of 'All Right Now'; on scratchy transistor radios, booming out of boutiques on a sunny Saturday afternoon, notes falling from house windows opened to breathe in the summer and let out the stuffiness, from the lowered glass of those few cars with fitted radios, from the speakers of a radio hung from the scaffolding of a building site, sung along to by labourers in between them wolf-whistling the girls. It was everywhere. This was their moment.

The financial rewards were considerable, especially to Fraser and Rodgers, the credited writers of the song. Island had seen to it that they had signed proper song-publishing deals as well as performing ones. There was now a very big surplus in their Island account and Andy, now with a licence allowing him to drive that Mercedes, made the long-overdue move out of his mum's council house.

I bought *Esgairs*, a 500-year old cottage in Horsell, a village a couple of miles outside of Woking, still only about an hour away from mum's. I bought it outright, didn't need to bother with a mortgage. The village was basically one high street with this cottage on it. It was quite historically famous, had been one of the first houses built there, at the bottom of the hill from the chapel. It had beautiful wooden beams and carvings, inglenook fireplaces and a tunnel from the house up to the chapel which the priests would use as a means of escape, I guess, during the dissolution of the monasteries a few hundred years ago. Some of the windows were bricked up from when there had been a windows tax, so it was like living history. It had a front extension built into it. The upstairs extension became the main bedroom of five and I made the downstairs extension into a studio. It was really, really nice. I went through that period of buying all this antique furniture and doing the place up. I was very excited by it all. It was the beginning of a different phase, I guess. I think we were all happy for each other – 'That's a nice car you've got, cool,' – but once you start living these separate existences, it changes everything. Especially when partners come along. Suddenly one's emotions are expressed and shared by an outside party as opposed to an inside party going through the songs. I just don't know if there is a way around that. It's inevitable, and even though plenty of bands have dealt with it and remained together, it is a big change and another one of those things that goes towards breaking bands up.

Although we were young guys who suddenly had access to a lot of money, we were pretty mature and intelligent. We weren't naive enough to assume that the flash cars, houses and drugs were being bought with the record company's money. Some bands think they're on a money train that's never going to run out and buy a dozen houses, three dozen cars and have tons of friends – really good friends! But we weren't like MC Hammer or Mick Fleetwood in that respect – going from owning a Hawaiian island to being bankrupt.

Later I bought mum her own house too, and a car. I felt really good about being able to do that because it was something that she'd long dreamt about. It was always her big ambition to have her own place and I was able to make it happen. She then got herself a boyfriend too and it was a happy time for her, I like to think.

A little later I began to get curious about my father. That ended with me turfing him out. He was a bit stunned obviously, grabbing his coat as I pushed him out the door in the middle of the night. I went back to bed and a couple of hours later I was awoken by the sound of pebbles hitting my window. I went to the window and there was a policeman with my father. He said, 'Your father here says he's left his wallet under the pillow.' I went to his room, found the wallet, threw it out the window and went back to bed. He must've walked the two miles into Woking and found the police station. That was the last time I saw him. No, not true: I actually saw him not long after that walking in a street in London when I was driving the car. I didn't stop. I had deleted him and I've never once regretted it.

He was – is – an incredibly arrogant man with a massive chip on his shoulder. I've heard lots of tales about him from my half-brother, one of the offspring of his marriage after mum, and they all tally to tell a very consistent tale of a conniving, self-serving, manipulative person. Sadly, my half-brother fell for it and suffered much more because of it. I'm just glad I worked it out as quickly as I did. My memories of him from childhood are vague. I remember everything had to be immaculate and he had a thing about white. Everything had to be white. He had a bright white car, this half-black guy, and he insisted mum and my sisters sat in the back, us males up front. It was the same when we were out walking – him up ahead, the rest of us had to stay behind, especially females. He's still the source of anger among my sisters and brother but I like to think I have no emotional attachment at all and can view it all in a detached way, even with some amusement.

There was little time back then to dwell on it. Free were gigging virtually non-stop, financially maximising their now universal popularity to scenes of 'Freemania' that usually required police escorts. Germany one moment, Sunderland the next, with more mass hysteria and a performance that left support act Deep Purple nervous about appearing in front of a crowd so rabidly wanting Free. One year on from the near-silence that greeted the end of their gig at Durham University (if that, indeed, is where 'All Right Now' was conceived) the same venue was witness to scenes of hysteria, 2,000 people squeezed into a hall, 1,000 more outside unable to get in, police trying to quell riots. The music press were dubbing them the new heirs to the throne of The Rolling Stones. Melody Maker reported scenes of 'Beatlemania-type Free-fever'. Any spare days squeezed from the schedule would be used to work in the studio, putting together their next album, Highway, to be released in December. Destination: the horizon. Nothing looked out of reach.

ALL RIGHT NOW

The success of 'All Right Now' sucked a hurricane of demands through a vortex and dumped them in the lap of the band, transporting them to a different level of existence. Island sensed the further flow of money ready to be tapped from their efforts and wanted a follow-up in short order, the song had gone to number one in several European territories which now needed to be toured to capitalise on that success – there was an expectation to live up to. Free had been on the road for three years, at their own pace, largely dictating their own terms. Now suddenly the outside world seemed to be dictating to them. Andy and the boys felt they had a clear vision of how Highway *should sound, and were in great shape spiritually, excited about the future, but their success meant the recording was being squeezed into a narrow window and there was, as yet, no obvious follow-up to 'All Right Now'. Then they listened as Koss, in between takes, doodled an addictively catchy riff on his guitar. Listen to the intro of the 'The Stealer' and that's what he was playing. The others looked at each other, instantly recognising the germ of something that sounded just the ticket.*

From that riff, we created and recorded the song in one day – we were on fire throughout the recording of that album. We finished recording 'The Stealer' in the early hours of the next morning and the engineer Andy Johns was so excited by it he ran up the stairs to Blackwell's apartment, banged on the door and said, 'Get down here and hear this.' To his credit Blackwell came down, heard it and said, 'Yep, that's a hit.' It was meant to be in a similar vein to 'All Right Now', but a little more alleyway as opposed to street, night time maybe rather than day, a little bit dirtier, darker. It's got a great groove and I really like it but looking back we didn't work it enough, it didn't have enough of a sing-along chorus for a single. We could easily have given it one had we devoted a bit more time to it. The whole focus for us at that time was playing live, the schedule was incredibly hectic. We'd be gigging right up to the night before a recording and straight afterwards. With *Highway* we didn't have as much stuff ready to take into the studio as previously, so it was even more time-compressed than usual. That extra bit of time for reflection could have been used to give 'The Stealer' what it needed to be a proper follow-up to 'All Right Now'. Maybe Blackwell was as swept along by the whole thing as we were, because his instincts were usually very good.

'The Stealer' was released as a single two months ahead of the album it came off and with expectations heightened by the monster that was 'All Right Now', it bombed, peaking no higher in the UK charts than number seventeen. To some in the band, this was felt as a major setback.

Paul R was very disappointed by that, and by how the album subsequently sold. It hit him really hard. I didn't really understand why and still don't. To me, it was no big deal, just took it in my stride, thought, 'Hey, we'll just write some more songs.'

It was perhaps the first indication of a divergence in the respective visions of Fraser and Rodgers. For Andy, so long as it was artistically valid, what did it matter where it charted, how many units were shifted? It wasn't as if the band wasn't more than paying for itself. For Rodgers, high on the success of 'All Right Now' and the Fire & Water *album, going from the crest of a wave to being ducked under the water didn't sit well. Commercial success, once tasted, was perhaps proving addictive. Given that these two were the creative heart of the group, this had worrying implications.*

Highway *lacks nothing in quality compared to the earlier albums but there was simply no big commercial hit single to light it up in the way that 'All Right Now' had lit up* Fire & Water. *The individual tracks within it rank among some of the band's finest work and show a continuing musical development. Andy had focussed* more on piano, less on bass, and the songs are structured around that. It's quieter, more introspective, an easy-going, more flowing dynamic that lends them a more American feel than before, but it's still recognisably the power house that is Free – it couldn't be anything else with Rodgers' voice and Koss's guitar. This phase of their work was in fact highly influential in America, creating the spark that brought Lynyrd Skynyrd into existence, for example. The album's title reflects the perspective from which it was created – constantly on the road – the relaxed vibe probably coming from their general easy mood regardless; they were still tight together in the midst of the madness, were enjoying the vindication and new-found security of their success. The greater piano emphasis didn't change the recognisably pared-down Free sound and as album tracks, the songs were as strong as ever. 'The Stealer' was the only 'in your face' power number, the rest a mixture of laid-back shuffle ('The Highway Song', 'On My Way', 'Bodie', 'Ride On A Pony') and familiar moody, beautiful Free ballad ('Be My Friend', 'Sunny Day', 'Love You So', 'Soon I Will Be Gone'). All were credited to the Fraser/Rodgers songwriting partnership apart from 'The Stealer' (which featured Kossoff in the credits too) and 'Love You So' (a joint effort between Kirke and Rodgers). Fraser continued to be the arranger, the one who constructed the sounds, though to this day Andy isn't sure if Rodgers ever fully understood the concept of arranging and therefore the value of this vital contribution.

Some of what I think was Paul Rodgers' best work was on there. 'Soon I Will Be Gone' stands out – it's one of my favourite Free songs and it has that folk balladeer quality that was such a wonderful part of him but which we'd never get to see again. I remember the recording well, felt it was rather an inspired day. Whenever we were playing, I was always right there, not thinking about yesterday, or worrying about tomorrow. That's what I really loved about the band. I assumed everyone felt the same. 'Love You So' was spearheaded by Simon and its ultra-sweet melodic sense is right in tune with his character. When this album was conceived we were all still in great spirits and the band was therefore in full health. When it was like this, any half-idea that anyone had was a good starting place and I really liked that concept – so much more than the subsequent one of Paul R's to lock ourselves into being a two-dimensional rock band. On this album we were still open to anything; for example 'Bodie', a song started by Paul and which I don't think quite works, was at least unusual and a bit out of character. Lyrically I never felt it was very relatable and I think a lesser singer than Paul couldn't have carried off the melody, but it was good for the fact that we tried it and didn't put barriers up.

During the recording of 'Soon I Will Be Gone', news came that Kossoff's idol Jimi Hendrix had died. Simon Kirke reckons it hit Koss so hard he was never quite the same again. The general mood was soon to darken further. Highway *was released in the UK in December 1970 and in the USA in February '71. It failed to chart in America and reached no higher than forty-one in the UK album charts even though the band was still attracting massive audiences and scenes of hysteria live. Many of the problems perhaps began there as Andy and Paul Rodgers assigned different levels of significance and reason for* Highway's *relative lack of success and how that impacted upon their future direction. They were still heavily on the touring treadmill, still trying to get into the studio on the rare gaps in the schedule, to pull together material for their next album. The tension between the pair began to tell.*

I think perhaps that's when the feeling first began to come from Paul that we'd tried it my way and it hadn't worked – though nothing was ever said, it was all vibe. For the first time there was the beginning of a feeling of us trying to pull in different directions. The fact that we were each beginning to write our own songs rather than collaborate on them, as we had previously, seemed to bring more tension too. I guess we were both pretty strong-willed and the atmosphere over the coming weeks and months began to get heavier. Poor Koss and Simon were caught in the middle of it. It didn't occur to me it was anything to do with *Highway's* performance, and I only later learned that had hit Paul so hard. But I think there was also the element of our personal lives developing along with our means. Your whole environment changes; you're suddenly buying houses with cash and you've all got cars, you're not living in your mother's house, the roadies are no longer sleeping on the floor next to you, no longer waking up and smoking joints together. There was a big difference between Paul sleeping on my mum's sofa and us having our own places further apart and, increasingly, our own lives. We were not communicating as well, we had a closer relationship with our girlfriends, we were no longer a gang of guys able to laugh together and see the silliness of it. Combine that with fame and it's a hard road to haul. You need to be a Sting or a Mick Jagger to have the intelligence to keep it in perspective – and we were teenagers. You are consistently tested and seduced and you have to pull back from it. Not getting swallowed up by it all is almost a bigger job than making the music. It boils down to celebrity-hood and you have to keep putting that aside, not be seduced by it and remember what it is that brought it, so the real artist in you survives. It takes some people a long time to get that and some never do.

Johnny Glover saw the dynamic changing from close-up: 'Andy had been the leader, no doubt about that, but somehow the marriage between him and Paul Rodgers just broke down. They changed as people. Paul's ego got bigger – and that's not a criticism, it comes with the territory of being the singer and he'd become a serious star. Andy's ego didn't, maybe because he'd always been the business side of the band and also not the front man. To successfully carry off the role of the front man in a majorly successful rock band you need a very healthy ego and Paul's definitely developed as Free became more successful. But Andy remained a very strong character and maybe those two things couldn't co-exist.'

Island – read Blackwell and Glover – were concerned about the disappointing sales of 'The Stealer' as the follow-up to 'All Right Now' and wanted to get another single out there quickly, to rescue the momentum, something catchy. So Andy wrote 'My Brother Jake', a sing-along, fairly lightweight song about a wayward brother. It was quickly recorded and pressed – and duly went to number four in the UK charts in early 1971. But that did little to ease the tensions. In fact it may even have intensified them in that Kossoff, keeper of the flame of authenticity, saw that single as a further move away from his love of the blues. Now Paul Rodgers evidently began to wonder if the steering of the band progressively further away from Koss's first love might not be connected with its reduced commercial success. If the band's Koss-centric live shows were still so hugely popular, he seemed to reason, let's go back to that on vinyl.

'My Brother Jake' came from hanging around with a black singer called Horace Faith, a great guy and great talent who lived on the street next to Alexis though he wasn't connected. I was trying to help him get established and was messing about musically with him. The song's kinda inspired by him but I just changed his name. It's just a song about a guy watching his life slip away – and pretty much everyone knows someone like that. We kind of just knocked it off, didn't really take it that seriously. I was on piano and I think if we'd done it a little more Motown without the bass pedal, disguising the fact there were so many chords, it could've been great. It ended up being OK in a sing-along, pub-song sort of way but could've been more. Partly this was about the very tight time constraints on us between all the touring but also it was about the dynamic between us, between me and Paul specifically, that somehow led us not to put as much effort into developing and recording the songs.

I felt Free had the potential to do many kinds of music and in my mind that could've combined commercial singles with far-out stuff in the way The Beatles had. They started off singing Little Richard and Chuck Berry songs but ended up doing 'A Day In The Life' and 'Across The Universe' and it was still commercial. The idea of us retreating back towards being just a blues-rock band was definitely not part of my vision but apparently it had become Paul's. The whole thing had always had a direction, a progression. Now he wanted to go backwards.

Things started to deteriorate between us, in the studio in particular, but also on the road. Johnny Glover really suffered during this time, trying to hold it all together. It put a lot of stress on Koss too, on top of all the musical stuff he was struggling with. The idea of being tightly knit began to come unravelled, I felt a real loss of camaraderie between Paul Rodgers and me, that he had developed his own agenda, but it wasn't one he ever articulated – not to me, anyway. All there was instead was a bad vibe, a downward spiral. In the middle of the intense schedule it just created an unbearable tension. It was no longer a happy place to be for any of us. We were dreading the Japan/Australia tour Johnny Glover had booked. I don't remember which of us first brought the idea of a split out into the open but once it had been said, there was general agreement. Certainly from my perspective, if we couldn't be moving on as a group, it was time for me to be moving on. We told Blackwell on the eve of the tour that we'd fulfil that obligation but thereafter we were calling it a day. No-one else knew at this stage.

Looking back on it now, it all seems to have buckled so suddenly: one moment at the top of the world, the next in total disharmony, all apparently triggered by slightly disappointing sales of an album. At just the point they had looked poised to become truly massive, instead they stumbled. That shouldn't have been a disaster in itself but it became so. From their youthful intensity things weren't being seen in their real perspective, only from the paranoia that now infected their fierce little unit. Maybe the strutting confidence of the front man Rodgers was actually a fragile thing – he was still only twenty-one years old, for chrissakes – and once that was damaged perhaps it triggered a fatal change in the whole dynamic of the group, in that Paul no longer trusted that Andy's instincts met with his own aims and Andy in turn didn't buy into Paul's alternative. Result: stalemate and festering, unspoken bitterness. Koss and Simon looked on from the sidelines, heartbroken.

Glover was somewhat startled by the news when Andy told him on the plane as they were flying to Japan, late April '71. 'Andy was sitting next to me,' he recalls, 'and said, "Well, everyone's a bit sad when things come to an end," and I asked him what he was talking about. And he said, "Oh, we're splitting up. Paul and I can't work together anymore." I said, "What you talking about? We've got a US tour after Australia, all booked." And Andy said, "No, we're not doing America. It's finished." They'd told Blackwell but Blackwell hadn't told me. I asked Simon about it afterwards and he was very mournful and confirmed it.'

Rodgers has gone on record with his side of the story in the Free biography Heavy Load *by David Clayton and Todd K Smith. 'I had made it clear to everyone that I wasn't ready to do an American tour straight after Japan and Australia,' he said. 'That was one of the frustrations. It was booked regardless and I thought, "Wow! I'm really not being listened to here." Everything was going along flat-out and you felt that you were on a big wheel turning and it was out of your control entirely, and that really brought it home to me: "Another tour, is everybody deaf?" I was not ready for it, and actually I'd just bought my cottage in the country and I needed to chill a little bit – sit back and take stock, that's really all I wanted, but I was so frustrated by the fact that it just went steaming ahead. They ignored anything I had to say about the subject so I said, "Right, I'm out." Another serious bone of contention would be that there came a time when I felt we needed to add more blues back into the set. We'd kept 'The Hunter,' made it our own, and I felt we could do the same with other blues songs – similar to what Zeppelin would do later. I could feel Koss's frustration at not being able to freewheel the material we'd been playing. Each attempt we made to play a blues song, Andy would either put his bass down and walk out, or deliberately sabotage it by playing like shit. His inflexibility seriously pissed me off. I tried on a number of occasions and then gave up. Andy had the idea that the band was his creation alone – playing the little emperor.'*

The idea of Paul wanting to do more covers like 'The Hunter' and be more like Led Zeppelin I think illustrates very clearly the differences building between us. I thought then, and still do, that was a ludicrous idea. But I really had no idea at the time that he was smouldering about the American tour. You can imagine in the years of touring everyone had their turns of being sick, or having pains, same as anyone else. But there was not a single instance I can think of when anyone said they couldn't make it that night. If one of us was sick it was just taken into consideration by the rest of us. Even later when Koss was whacked out he never said he couldn't make it and in fact did his best. No-one ever made excuses and there were many nights Paul sang despite having a terrible cold or the 'flu. So to hear later that the biggest macho man in the band wanted out because he was tired just doesn't compute.

I don't recall ever deliberately playing badly. As for the 'playing the little emperor', hmm, I find that an interesting choice of words – very Asian, Japanese, as was his new wife. People tend to 'walk on eggshells' around Paul and when someone doesn't it tends to ruffle the feathers. I felt it had always been 'us' not just 'me' but now suddenly Paul had decided it was his way or the highway and just communicated with me with a kind of blankness, like I wasn't really there. I'd always felt one of my functions was to be a cohesive factor, create a space where everyone could be free to express themselves naturally. Imagine an orchestra, and the conductor says, 'Just play the blues, man.' It ain't gonna work. Someone needs to say, 'This is the song, you take this space, you take that space, and do what comes naturally within it,' only in a much less rigid, more free-form way than with an orchestra. It was essential to include everyone, we just all needed to be on the same page.

Although Koss had some difficulty with that direction, I never felt it was because he didn't like it, just that it was different to his original expectation of just playing blues and that he had to learn new stuff. But, unbeknown to me, Paul Rodgers had decided we were doing something else and instead of camaraderie, I was being re-cast as just the bass player, a sideman. All without saying anything, including his gripes about the US tour. It became intolerable.

Personally I think he'd already moved out in his head. When he says, 'Right, I'm outta here,' that's exactly how it felt at the time, like he'd already moved on, maybe to a band where everyone just did as he told them. Suddenly he felt 'lack of control', something that in the past didn't bother him, in fact allowed him to be the great artist he was, but he had lost trust. One can't demand trust, just accept, if it's not there, time to move on. Now he turned 180 per cent into a 'control freak' and a streak of manipulation began growing. Actually, it's not as though I don't understand, without judgment, given what was going on, why this came to be. Survival mode set in, and that was his way of dealing with it.

Success can be measured in many ways; artistic, skill, financial, commercial, performance, creative. Keeping these in balance is a tricky thing, and for a while we were lucky enough for them all to be happening at the same time. It's easy to understand when times are tough sometimes the artistic can take second place to the need to appear successful, in commercial terms. We all make choices and have to live with them. I suppose everyone's perception is valid and one of the dangers inherent in becoming bigger and bigger is we all become monsters – even to each other.

In hindsight it's clear that Paul's direction was moving to what subsequently became Bad Company, basically a two-dimensional rock band. He was closing down that balladeer side of himself, the part I thought needed to be brought out more. I thought we could have moved way beyond blues rock, that there was nothing we couldn't try and we all had the potential to stretch out in other directions; but to do that meant freeing everyone up, not locking ourselves into these stock roles like his 'Clint Eastwood of rock' persona. I guess he still does a pretty good Chuck Norris! But in the meantime I feel we've lost out on a lot of great stuff. I think we definitely cut ourselves short.

Simon Kirke has recalled the day he heard the news that Free were disbanding: 'We were in the final mixing sessions of Highway,' he said, 'I think it was one of the last sessions, and me and Koss walked in - I was living with Koss at the time. We only lived around the corner from Island Records. We walked in and Andy and Paul were already there, doing some mixes. And I remember the engineer looking at me and Koss and sort of rolling his eyes, and I remember Andy saying, "Listen, we've got to talk. After this tour and this album, me and Paul want to go our own ways."

'And I couldn't believe what I was hearing. It was just unbelievable. And that was it really. We thought maybe it was just something they were going through. We'd get Chris Blackwell in on it, and we'd sit down around a table and talk about it like grown men. But it never happened. And that's exactly what happened — a big shame. That's really when Koss went in a downward spiral, because he lived for the band. He loved Paul's voice. I don't think he saw himself working with any other band. And quite frankly, neither did I.'

It's since been said that we just needed to take a break rather than split up – and maybe there's some truth in that. Certainly, part of why The Rolling Stones have stayed together so long is, I'm sure, they just never announced they'd split – even when things were bad and they had in reality split. Then after a time it all got resolved somehow. Maybe that's what we should have done, though I'm not convinced.

The only person maybe strong enough to have got us to do that would have been Blackwell but even with him whenever we wanted to say no to him we would. But he had our respect and perhaps if he'd suggested such a thing we would have listened. But here's a funny thing about Chris: he finds potential young stars and builds them into stars and they then become stars in his mind. Whereas someone like Berry Gordy would say to Marvin Gaye, 'You're going on tonight,' slap him across the face and brook no dissent, Blackwell would never force his artists into doing anything, even if he believed it was for their own good. Part of what allowed you to flourish with him was he didn't put parameters up and maybe that disallowed him from saying, 'Do this, do that.' Maybe he credits young artists with too much maturity.

'The performances the band gave In Japan and Australia were quite sensational,' says Glover. 'They really went out on a high. They were selling out big stadiums, with thousands unable to get in and then they would put on a mind-blowing show. I think the tension between them actually added to their performance.'

I agree. The tension, frustrations and anger between us fuelled our energy on stage. We channelled it into the shows and we were monstrous, maybe the best we'd ever played. Some of the scenes in Japan were extraordinary – playing to massive arenas with thousands of people unable to get in, fans that were, if anything, even more hysterical than in the UK. But after the show we'd go our separate ways, in separate cars. Paul Rodgers met a Japanese girl, Machi, who subsequently became his wife. Koss hung out with a Japanese musician Tetsu Yamauchi, who would later figure in the band's story. I picked up a Japanese girlfriend out there too – or rather she picked me up. She was very well placed and determined to get her way – and she did, for our whole stay.

Then it was off to Australia, and our most bizarre tour of all. The promoter was there to meet us off the plane in Perth and he took us to the waiting coach and our bags were loaded but he seemed nervous as hell, sweating like a wet fish. Something was seriously amiss – this guy seemed like he was about to have a seizure. What the hell was he so worried about? It soon became clear. Basically he had been kidnapped by a gangster called Sammy Lee and his hoods who were now running the tour, with the ex-promoter as just the front man.

Sammy Lee was a Sydney-based club owner with 'close connections' to organised crime. He owned the Les Girls club in the Kings Cross part of the city, drag queens singing, miming and dancing. At another of his clubs a local gangster was shot dead in 1967. Sammy Lee was right in the middle of the gang wars that were part of the entertainment industry there at that time. By 1971 he was just four years from the end of his life, an unhealthy-looking fifty-nine years old, fat, balding, pencil moustache, face as hard as nails, a firecracker just waiting to go off. Amid all the menace, he'd sometimes try to be pally with the artists, play the magnanimous host, parade the famous showbiz names as his friends in front of his clientele, just like the clichéd gangster he was.

One night we were invited to go out to some drag show, so I guess that would have been his place. I declined as I never found drag entertaining. In fact years later as I struggled to come to terms with being gay, that was one of the things I kept coming back to – 'How can I be gay? I fucking hate drag shows.'

Luckily for us, Johnny Glover had already done his deal with the original promoter and had secured fifty per cent of our fee in advance. But we were part of a bill with Manfred Mann and Deep Purple and I'm not sure if their management had been so efficient.

It didn't really affect us; we just did our shows as normal. But there was one day when we were riding to the hotel in the bus with everyone. We were a bit stoned and Koss went into one of his funny characters and said mockingly, with his hand to his brow, 'Oh, I'm so stressed, I don't know if I can go on today,' and one of the hoods pulled a gun and said, 'Oh yes you can.' Actually it was quite funny, the idea that this guy just didn't realise it was only a joke. We just sort of looked at each other and shrugged our shoulders. Again we played to huge audiences. Our final gig at Sydney's Randwick Racecourse was in front of about 50,000 people but there were about that many outside unable to get in. It occurred to Sammy Lee at this point that he could put us all on again and sell out twice. Johnny Glover got wind of this and made sure there were cars waiting for us as soon as we came off, ready to whisk us away to the airport. But Manfred Mann's manager got the shit beat out of him when he refused to send them on again after their first performance and was quite badly injured.

'It was very sad,' says Glover. 'It was over. I shared a car to the airport with Koss and Simon. Andy and Paul were in separate cars. They were all going to different places – Andy back to the UK, Paul back to Japan, Simon over to the States, Koss back to Japan too. Simon looked at me and said, "It's a weird moment, isn't it?" I don't think Koss and Simon thought they were ever going to do anything other than be the guitarist and drummer in Free and when it all came apart they were devastated. Simon was a lighter personality than Koss so he was able to survive OK but Koss really stewed and ground himself down. That's when his drugs problems really began – although I only found that out some time later.'

Andy Fraser, eighteen-year-old superstar and millionaire, flew home to apparent oblivion.

It hurt. This had been the love of my life and now suddenly it was over, just switched off. It's one of the heartbreaks in my life that we didn't reach the potential I think we had; we'd only just started. So yes I was heavily down in the aftermath. But I couldn't have continued with it the way it was going, none of us could. If it wasn't happening it was better to be real about it than continually suffer it not happening and being in the middle of it, which was just awful. We'd had this thing that was so magical but you just had to accept that it didn't feel magical any more. So in one sense there was a relief it was over, but you can't just switch off the sad feelings. That had been my family and now it was gone.

I went back to *Esgairs* and continued to work on new songs, which gave me something to do in the immediate aftermath. I had the idea of getting a new band together, finding another family, but one in which I would sing this time. My lyrics and song writing had developed and I needed something that would bring that out more. I realised I really needed to develop my voice if I was to do that, and though it represented a huge challenge – that was something I needed. I guess it would have been possible to hook up with some other well-known musicians and make a 'supergroup' but that had no appeal. I was thinking, 'Where do I go to get real again, to find a situation in which I could have artistic success and development as well as commercial success?' It was a process of a couple of months getting re-grounded, settling into the house, writing new stuff, just somehow finding my equilibrium again. Chris Blackwell was very supportive and encouraging whenever we spoke, but that wasn't so often. He had a business empire to run, had homes in several countries, would only be in the UK for three weeks at a time.

I was also speaking regularly with Alexis and after I told him I wasn't into getting a supergroup together but was more into getting fresh, keen, new musicians and starting again he told me about Stan Speake, this young drummer he'd played with from Wales who he really reckoned. I'd also hooked up with a young guitarist, Adrian Fisher, through an ad. He was very naturally gifted and later was in the band Sparks. I googled him recently and found that he'd died back in 2000. We should be thankful for every day we have. The three of us began rehearsing in the studio at the cottage. I had to learn not only to sing but to sing and play bass at the same time – which is no easy thing at first and the reason why singing bassists like Paul McCartney or Sting are such a rarity. The name of the band was Toby – which was a nickname our Free roadie Graham Whyte had given me, said I reminded him of a 'Toby Jug' of New Zealand ale. We eventually recorded a whole album's-worth of songs – including one called 'Travelling Man' – but it was canned, as events rather overtook it.

Although Toby ended up not going anywhere it was incredibly important from my point of view. I had to learn to be a singer, to stick my neck out and find out what it was like. Having Paul Rodgers as a yardstick didn't exactly make it easy and the end product fell a bit short because my singing wasn't yet up to scratch but the songs were good. You may say, 'Why the hell leave the band with the world's best singer to form one where I couldn't even sing?!' But it was a valuable experience, much more so than joining a supergroup would have been. I think Paul Rodgers went through a similar process in improving his guitar playing with the band he formed, Peace.

In the middle of this, my mum died. It came very suddenly. I went round to visit her at the house one day and couldn't get an answer. She eventually came to the door looking like death and complaining of a terrible headache. Within two weeks she was *non-comprende* to the world, within four she was dead. The first doctor had said, 'Take two of these, call me in the morning,' but the next one had her straight into hospital where she was diagnosed with a brain tumour.

I was due in court for a traffic speeding offence on the morning I'd been told she'd died. I sat there completely numb as the judge told me how he was taking my driving licence from me and I was 'a stupid young man' – and him sitting there with what looked like a sheepskin on his head. I refrained from comment.

For a long time – a few years – I carried this idea around that, somehow mum's death was my fault. I had this weird idea that everyone has something they want to accomplish in life and once they get there they die. Mum had always wanted her own house and I'd helped her realise her dreams so she'd completed her mission. It was nonsense of course, but that didn't stop it being in the back of my mind for a long time. I'd always felt very tenderly towards her and it was a very tough time.

Mother gone, band gone, father 'deleted'. Even for such an independent spirit, it can only have left the nineteen-year-old Andy starkly bereft. It just adds to the enormity of experience squeezed into his short, compressed life. His talk of wanting to 'keep it real' in this time of turmoil is very characteristically him. He's still real now, the most natural and unassuming host you could possibly imagine. I know people with a tiny fraction of his accomplishments with much more of a 'front', that transmitting of a certain status, than him. There is absolutely no 'I'm Andy Fraser' about him, something that Johnny Glover touched on when describing the reasons for the Fraser/Rodgers partnership dissolving. When Andy talks of the pitfalls of the superficially-inviting celebrity and how aware he was of them and how continually on his guard against them he was, it all tallies. When Glover talks of how Paul Rodgers' ego developed with the success of the band – and of how necessary it is to have that egocentric core when you are fronting a major rock band – so it makes sense not only of the changing internal dynamics of the band according to how successful it was, but also the situations in which the individual members found themselves in the wake of its dissolution. Andy's lack of desire to form a supergroup, which might have enabled him to maintain the commercial momentum of Free, should be seen in this context of staying real. A supergroup with the egos of the other members already rampant was the last place he needed or wanted to be. But that he still needed 'a family' was hardly surprising, hence the search for a new one.

A few miles to the east, in London, one of the other band members was struggling rather more than Andy with the conflicts, both of celebrity and those arising from the breaking up of the band. Paul Kossoff was in a bad way. More than any of the others, Free had been his family. He'd once said in an interview: 'The life revolves around the music. If the music's not good for any reason then life is just toned down. It's the only life I know, the only existence I've hit upon.' Kirke – the band member closest to Koss – had noticed his appetite for pills had increased during the last few difficult months of Free, though not to the extent that it was affecting his playing or his personality. He'd become partial to Mandrax. In the aftermath of the break-up, his intake was to increase and broaden dramatically. He'd excommunicated his family after rowing with his father David about his state. In place of family and band members, hangers-on and drug pushers moved in, a horrible vicious circle.

I think Koss felt especially vulnerable after we split. In the band he'd been covered, protected, from his insecurities as a player. Although he did what he did fantastically well, with such emotion and conviction, he was actually quite a basic player. Yet because of how well he did what he did in the band, and how fantastic he was live, he'd built up this big reputation and people were talking of him in the same breath as the guitar greats – Hendrix, Peter Green, Eric Clapton. These guys were Koss's heroes and he didn't, in his heart of hearts, believe he was worthy of comparison to them. So when you took the band away I think there was a real feeling of vulnerability and I think the terrible consequence of that was his drug intake. Koss was looking for a way out I think. It had all fallen apart. He didn't feel confident that the fame and adulation being poured on him were justified and with the band falling apart he had no-one to lean on. I think somewhere in his mind he followed in the footsteps of his heroes like Hendrix and the other drug people. If people saw him on stage and he was bad then the excuse was it was because he was drugged – as opposed to he was bad. It's a weird psychological thing. I think he wanted out and it was like a slow suicide.

One of our roadies, Jim McGuire, who had stayed with me throughout all the breakups, had told me about the state Koss had got into. I'd been around to see him and it was pitiful. In the wake of 'All Right Now' he'd bought this little place in Golborne Mews, near Portobello market. Blackwell had originally bought it, fixed it up, but when Koss expressed an interest in it, he sold it to him in a pretty good deal. This was where I went. It was just two rooms basically, one upstairs and one downstairs, connected by a spiral staircase. You walked in the door and the place was just full of druggies, completely out of it, looked like hundreds of them lying on the floor, leaning against the walls. Koss was upstairs, surrounded by more of them, handing him stuff, and was just making no sense at all, just fucked, hardly knew his own name. Who knows what he was on – everything. When you're in that stage between 'mandies' and heroin, all sorts of other stuff tends to get included; 'Hey, have a hit of coke to wake you up, Koss,' or 'Ooh, look what I've got for you today, Koss.' All these low-lifes leeching off him. It was horrible.

Jim and I agreed we had to get him out of there. We stepped over the bodies and basically kidnapped him. He was too out of it to resist and so was everyone else. We drove him down to *Esgairs* in Surrey where there was nowhere for him to go. Over the next few days we tried to talk to him, cajole him, reason with him, saying, 'If you're in there, Koss, we're trying to reach you.' But there was nothing we could do. He resented being there and didn't want to be helped. In the end we just had to take him back, which gave us a horrible feeling of failure. It was like finding a baby in a dumpster, rescuing it then putting it back in the dumpster after a few days. It felt criminal placing him back in such a bad environment. This was in the days before rehab, before addiction was properly understood, but even with that understanding if you don't want to be helped there is no helping you – and that's how it was at that time with Koss.

Word had got back to Johnny Glover about Koss's state too. It set in motion a train of events that was to have significant consequences: 'I think it was one of the engineers who first told me about Koss's problems, maybe 'Diga' [Richard Digby-Smith]. It was unusual in that it was pills. Everyone smoked dope, then there was heroin – you didn't see cocaine around then. But with Koss it was pills and that was unusual. I'd been looking after both Peace and Toby, neither of which blew me away; neither were as good as Free. Blackwell was in the West Indies. The Peace and Toby tours were over, both had finished recording. Simon and I chatted about the situation and I just thought, "I'm going to talk to the others." I went to Andy, talked about the state of Koss and said, "Look, we never did a farewell tour, why not do that to try and pull Koss out of it," and Andy said, "Well if Paul R says yes, then OK." I went to see Paul and we chatted and agreed. I think at some point Andy and Paul talked and they agreed to do it for Koss. Blackwell got wind of it all, phoned me up and said, "What the fuck are you up to?" and I explained and he said, "OK, fine."'

Yes, the number one reason for getting back together was Koss. But the fact that Toby and Peace weren't going anywhere also helped a lot. It was obvious to us and everyone else they weren't going anywhere apart from giving us those valuable experiences. The bottom line was we were all so aware of Koss slipping so fast and without anything else pulling us in another direction, it seemed the obvious thing to do: if we got back together it would stop Koss from slipping, give him a reason to pull out of this very fast downwards slide. It was a decision that was staring us in the face, really. We'd had almost a year apart and that horribleness of the last few months of Free before the breakup had faded in the memory, I guess.

Although Glover had couched it as just a farewell tour, for the band members themselves it was always meant to be more than that – once the decision had been made to reform. 'Koss was so happy,' recalls Glover. 'He was saying, "This is all I ever wanted."' Ironically, it had been Kossoff – together with Kirke – who'd successfully completed an album during Free's hiatus, Kossoff, Kirke, Tetsu and Rabbit, *a nice bit of work with Koss's guitar at its centre, in full flower without the constraints of Free, but also without Free's strong songwriting. He may have been out of it for much of the time, but he'd still managed to play extensively. It's been reported the others were shocked when they regrouped and saw how far Koss had fallen physically, but they'd all been in the loop as it happened and were more than aware of the rebuilding job ahead of them. Certainly Andy had seen him during the very depths when he'd tried the kidnap and at least the guitarist was now in better shape than that, buoyed by the band's rebirth.*

Ironically, in Free's absence the band had grown bigger. When UK tour dates were announced for early '72, they sold out almost instantly and the band would go on to break many UK venue attendance records – including some held by Led Zeppelin. More dates were hurriedly added and the crowd hysteria started from where it had left off last time.

It was OK at first, but a little uncertain, just like you'd imagine if you'd been through a trauma. I guess it was nice to be back on one level but it didn't yet feel like the robust, strong unit it had been at its best. Obviously Koss and whether he would pull himself straight was now the concern. It lent the whole thing a sense of fragility.

One of the early gigs in the UK tour was at London's Royal Albert Hall. I'd been messing about with a tune earlier that day called 'Little Bit Of Love' and I recall saying to the others backstage, 'Listen, I think I've got something going here,' and playing them what I had. Then we rehearsed a few things from our set. Koss seemed fine beforehand but as soon as we started playing on stage it was obvious something was badly wrong. He was five minutes behind us in what he was playing; we looked at each other, the audience looked at each other. You could see people in the crowd crying for him, wishing it would be all right. You cannot imagine what that is like when you're up there playing – we just wanted to curl up and die. But if it was bad for me, it must have been infinitely worse for Paul Rodgers. To be fronting a band with all those thousands and thousands looking on, and knowing it was so bad. We could at least just turn our amp up, but the singer is completely exposed – then the awful silence afterwards. There are not many who could stand up in front of a load of trash like that and still convince you they are a good singer. I think that incident may have had major implications on PR's attitude later when he was putting Bad Company together. That experience would have been enough.

Once he'd been through that nightmare, I can see why he would want low maintenance and sturdy rather than creative but high maintenance.

I was devastated as I got in the car to drive back home. The night had started so well, I was feeling really optimistic, I was excited by the new song that was coming together – and then this. I don't know what Koss had taken in between rehearsing and going on stage, or whether he'd taken something earlier and it had taken a while to kick in. Whatever, it had made us look pitiful, something that was very painful to take.

On his way back, Paul Rodgers stopped by at my place – it was sort of on his way home to Guildford – and we worked some more on 'Little Bit of Love'. He came up then with that great verse, 'Well, in my mind, it's easy, to lose sight of the truth'. That was a moment of pure inspiration, opening himself up to the universe and it was a special moment, I felt. I remember thinking, 'Yes, that's the Paul I love. That's the one I want to see more of.' But it was difficult to know which way it was all going, given what we'd just seen with Koss.

As we continued with the tour, it seemed Koss was making a real effort and for the most part he did OK. There were moments where he was back to or close to his best. It made you think, 'OK, this might just work out.'

As ever, studio time was squeezed in between the gigs. Andy brought some of his Toby songs, most notably 'Travelling Man', while Rodgers brought a few he'd written for Peace. These would form the backbone of Free At Last *, the band's comeback record, their fifth studio album. There seems to have been a real effort to allow Kossoff more space to express himself, his guitar less constrained than in previous Free LPs and developing in its sound too.*

In the interests of creating a feeling of unity, Rodgers had suggested all songwriting credits be shared between the four of them. The recording hits heights comparable to the pre-breakup albums – 'Little Bit Of Love', the mournful Rodgers-penned 'Child' – but somehow the uncertain circumstances are felt. There's a feeling of tentativeness about it; there's a fragile magic in it but it's not as sharply defined and there's little of the previous strutting confidence. The musical development audible in the sequence of previous albums definitely veers off here; the flowing tumble of Highway *is not present, nor the white soul of* Fire & Water. *In its place is just a variation on the band's core, with more extensive use of Kossoff's guitar but otherwise it's not really going anywhere. It's an album that has its fierce defenders among the legions of Free fans, but if Paul Rodgers had the aim of reeling in Andy's musical ambition, he succeeded here. It represents the full-stop to that ambition. Who knows, it might have been simply a punctuation, a pause for creative breath, were it not for the complicating matter of Kossoff's addiction, which rather took the energy away from everyone, creative or otherwise.*

It kicks off with a stuttering boogie from Andy, 'Catch A Train', followed by the evocative Rodgers' 'Soldier Boy'. Then it's Andy's bluesy 'Magic Ship' and Rodgers' slow 'Sail On' before Andy's Toby composition 'Travelling Man' and the co-written but Andy-initiated 'Little Bit Of Love'. Two deeply introspective Rodgers numbers, 'Guardian Of The Universe' and 'Child' come before the appropriately named sign off from Andy, 'Goodbye'.

I wrote 'Catch A Train' during the split. There was a train to Woking from London and someone was coming out to visit, maybe Robert Palmer who didn't drive, and I'd been giving instructions about which train to get. I'd known Robert for ages, back when he was Alan Robert Palmer. Then he got signed by Island as part of Vinegar Joe. He had a flat near Hampstead Heath and I'd go round there a lot. He turned me on to Marvin Gaye. He was a wonderful, sweet, open guy but a serial substance-abuser and I think he'd decided it was probably in his best interests that he didn't learn to drive. Anyway, that's how 'Catch A Train' was triggered. 'Soldier Boy' really displays an element of Paul Rodgers which I love; if I believed in reincarnation, that's what he'd have been. The fact that he'd come up with that inspired moment on 'Little Bit Of Love' just when we were right in the middle of despair about Koss at the Albert Hall was typical of him, going on regardless, dead and dying all around him, an unstoppable force. I really like 'Sail On' too, considering the shit we were going through. 'Travelling Man' was just a reflection of always being on the road and the words just fitted the riff.

Being in the studio at this time with Koss presented its challenges. He would just suddenly fall asleep at his guitar! We would go and do our parts separately for solos or overdubs. Koss would go off ready to do a take and next moment he'd just be sound asleep. He could still do it in short bursts, but it was really a strain for him. Those riffs he does on 'Little Bit Of Love' sound great, but boy was it hard work for him that day, a real burst of energy and inspiration. I can remember the rest of us huddled in the control room saying, 'Yeah, go on, Koss, you can do it,' and really getting behind him. Other times we'd be discussing something and he'd just have nodded off. You kind of felt lost for words. It was awful really. There wasn't much of the old, funny Koss left, just the odd moment. Most of the time life wasn't fun anymore and I think he felt as much of a burden as he was – and that can't have been nice. We'd done this to help and he was trying to respond but couldn't and was just left feeling guilty and with no way out. Afterwards he'd convince you that it wouldn't ever happen again but it always did.

It wasn't only Koss either. The old problems between me and Paul Rodgers that had split us up the first time hadn't really gone away. As well as our differing musical visions he was also starting to talk about getting some management that 'would break some legs' to get us better deals. I think he'd been very much seduced by how Peter Grant operated for Led Zeppelin, but I wanted no part of that kind of operating.

Then things escalated during the recording of Paul's song 'Guardian Of The Universe'. Paul was by now married to Machi and their son Stephen had just been born. This song was a lullaby and his prayer to the universe to look after the child – such a powerful subject and what a great title. It was a truly beautiful song too. Except it got murdered! He sang and played rather heavy-handed piano first, then said, 'OK, Kirkie, why don't you stick some drums on,' and Simon was drumming like a sergeant major, an arrangement that was just totally inappropriate for this slow, beautiful song. I couldn't believe what I was hearing, murdering this unbelievable song in front of my eyes and I thought, 'If you're doing this to your own song there's really no fucking hope.' I was suggesting things, trying to soften it, trying all sorts of bass parts to help but no matter what I did it still sounded like a hippo in labour pain. I would say, 'But can't you hear we're murdering it?' and Paul would just look through me. He was in 'I'm the man of the household and I have a wife and kids to take care of and I'm in charge' mode and was back to treating me like a session musician – 'Just play the bass and be quiet.'

Being the family man was just another of those things coming between us. Machi had married Paul, not the band, and while she was always very courteous I'm not even sure she really knew who I was. If the blonde guy was Simon, I must be Andy. She couldn't speak English at that stage either, so it was all a bit strange. You had no idea whether she'd understood what you'd said. Often she would just reply, 'Imagine,' which could have meant anything, very non-committal, and seemed a very Japanese thing. I've often wondered if that's what sparked John Lennon's song of that name – Yoko probably said it all the time.

With Paul I was talking to a blank page. It's easy for me to have perspective on him and maybe it's easier for him to have perspective on me now but it seemed he'd become a completely different person and I think there was no going back from that.

It was apparent that there was no point having me around if he didn't want what I had to offer. I think we'd both agreed it wasn't working – either between us or with Koss. But we still had the American tour we'd committed to. There was still the hope it might work but increasingly it was looking like this was going to be the last thing we did. You have to remember we had been this outfit that could rely totally on each other, the four of us formed this great partnership, a bit like a crack commando team that had got used to doing successful 'hit and runs' every night, watching each other's back, trusting the integrity of the unit. Then suddenly one of the team starts pulling imaginary spider's webs from his face, and you never knew when it was going to happen next. It made us all jumpy and we stepped out of our roles. I'm sure Paul's 'I'm in charge now' was partly a defence mechanism to that, partly a reflection of moving into a new phase of his life as a married father.

'Goodbye' was something I wrote in the middle of all this and with a fairly self-explanatory title. It was written about the shape we were in and to the rest of them about us and, I'd like to think, was written in a generous-spirited way. It was an obvious choice as the last song on what was now going to be our last album.

The US tour was when it really began to fall apart with Koss. It was like being in the middle of a bad movie. The nightmare element became intensified with the death of Jim McGuire, my roadie and friend, the guy who'd stayed with me through the split, who'd helped me kidnap Koss. We'd been doing a show and the three roadies would then pack up, load the rented U-Haul truck and drive it to the next venue. There was a sleeping area behind the cab and Jim, who was the most lovely guy, had gone to get his head down. When they stopped and went to wake him, he was dead from carbon monoxide poisoning from the exhaust. It was just awful and together with the stresses we were going through in the band, and Koss's problems, it made the whole experience quite horrific.

Finding Koss out of it on the hotel bathroom floor on the very first day we were due to be performing at The Palladium in LA summed it all up really. In the wake of that we had to cancel a few dates and Blackwell suggested we come down to his place in Nassau. We all went there and coming through customs they found a grass seed in Simon's suitcase. It was a briefly shaky moment but in the end they just fined him $300 and let him go. At other borders we had carried stuff through and were probably lucky we hadn't got ourselves into a whole heap of trouble.

We had a great time just hanging out at Blackwell's place recuperating and one day he took us all water skiing on his boat. I'd never done it before, but it was all going pretty well. I got up on my first try and didn't fall down for ages, hanging on as if my life depended on it – which it did actually, because I couldn't swim! As I eventually fell off I notified everyone of my lack of swimming ability. Blackwell shoved Glover over the side of the boat, saying, 'Save him, quick,' and Johnny duly rescued me.

But there was no rescuing the band; I think we all saw that. Koss's problems were too big for the band to rescue and in many ways it just increased the pressure on him. It meant the whole thing imploded without Koss's vital part of the whole. We each tried to compensate but that just led to more conflict as we were stepping out of the natural roles we'd assumed and which had the magic chemistry that had previously worked so well. Koss tends to get given the blame for Free's demise but actually which came first, the chicken or the egg? He maybe withdrew into the drugs as a result of the tensions between me and Paul Rodgers the first time around.

'Koss's problems really only became serious after the band split the first time,' says Glover. 'By the time it reformed he was too far gone. I'm no psychologist but it seemed to me the drugs had created a split personality in Koss. There was this demonic Koss that created all the awful scenes but then when he came out of it he'd be distraught and you'd see the old Koss. A second personality had been created which he could not control – and his body was deteriorating too. It was heart-breaking to see and Andy was the first to bail out, the first to say, "I can't handle this anymore."'

When we returned from the States, that was it. There was no band, it was over. In the press it was reported that I had left, but in fact it had been my job to report that we had broken up. It wasn't the time to split hairs – never is actually. So much is written inaccurately one would go nuts trying to rectify it. But because it was reported as me leaving, it gave Paul the room to manoeuvre, to create another band with replacements and call it 'Free'. I suppose I could have made some legal tussle over the name, as so many bands do, but it is just ugly, pitiful, and I didn't want to go there. I felt it would collapse of its own weight, which it did very shortly afterwards.

Free did indeed lurch through the rest of '72 and into '73 – but minus Andy and, often as not, minus Kossoff too on account of his health. Rodgers and Kirke stayed put and two of the musicians from Kossoff's and Kirke's earlier project – the bassist Tetsu Yamauchi and keyboards man 'Rabbit' Bundrick – were brought in. This line-up, plus session contributions from Kossoff, recorded the Heartbreaker *album. Later personnel additions – Snuffy Walden (who could play a passable impersonation of Kossoff) and Wendell Richardson – were made to bolster the band's perilous state. But even without Andy, the meltdown of the band continued regardless and it duly died early in '73. A feel of the 'going on regardless' strength of Paul Rodgers can perhaps be glimpsed from a line in the song 'Heartbreaker', title track of the only Fraser-less Free album: 'Burning my own eyes out to make a new start, to reach the goal.' He didn't have it any easier once Andy had left.*

Heartbreaker? Rhymes with Andy Fraser. Or is that just paranoia on my part? That album has a sense of doom about it, that I suppose was being felt by all within the band at the time. My suspicion is that Rabbit, being the kind of musician he is, took one look at things and thought, 'What a mess,' and tried to get things better organised and tried to get some structure into the arranging and my guess is that Paul then thought, 'Oh no, not another emperor,' because their tour descended into actual fist fights between the two of them – blood and broken fingers sort of stuff. I wasn't at all surprised when it ended the way it did.

It really was over now. Rodgers would later hook up with Led Zeppelin's manager Peter Grant, taking Simon Kirke and Mott the Hoople's Mick Ralphs with him to form Bad Company. Grant did his magic, threatened to break legs, got them a huge advance – and the band's 1974 debut album went to number one in America. Paul Rodgers now had the vast commercial success he'd craved – and with a dependable, tour-worthy outfit that could hit hard with the minimum of hassle. It did powerful, sing-along, stadium-friendly anthems like 'Can't Get Enough' and 'Feel Like Makin' Love' but it was a three-chord rock band, no matter how it's dressed up. There was precious little of Free's vulnerable magic about it.

'I think ultimately Island wasn't then a big enough organisation to make Free as big as they could have become,' says Glover today. 'They could have had what Zeppelin had if they'd had the necessary support. They were briefly that big but it couldn't be sustained. That's essentially why I left – I could see Island's limitations and I wanted to become a manager. Island was a label and a management company and Free were contracted to both and it was very, very tightly budgeted. I wasn't even allowed an external PR, for example. But there were acts we had on the label that were managed

by outside people and they always got much bigger promotional support – like Roxy Music, for example, who, with respect, were not in the same league.'

Although Island was supportive vibe-wise, maybe they didn't then have the facilities to really give a band a deeper level of support than just that. I know that when U2 joined they had a manager that came with the band and he seems to have been integral to keeping them together and maybe helping them through all those tough periods. We never did. In the States a record company isn't allowed to manage or be an agency as well. With Island it was a record company, a booking office, a management agency, an all-inclusive deal. We had Johnny who looked after us on Island's behalf but we didn't have a full-time guy looking after just our interests. Blackwell was great but as a sharp guy running a big company, he was only around some of the time. You need a manager you converse with every day and perhaps that's what we lacked.

In an idealised alternative history, Island might have made the necessary investment to give Free the commercial success Paul Rodgers wanted without compromising Andy's creative ambitions, the band could thereby have met both sets of expectations, it wouldn't have broken up and Kossoff wouldn't have descended into drug oblivion and ultimately death and the world would be enriched. But could that have happened? Would it? Or was Free's delicate beauty derived in part from the very flaws in its make-up that ensured it could not last? Were those wistful minor keys the very sound of a fractured soul? Vulnerability and bravado, that heart-breaking combination, and the inevitability of where it leads; it was all there in the songs.

'I loved that band,' says Blackwell. 'It was the first band I felt so protective of, like they were my kids, but ultimately I couldn't protect them. They were one of the greatest bands ever. Had they stayed together they would have been huge.'

Even forty years on, it's pretty clear Andy still holds a candle for what it was, before the difficult days. Not in the sense of wishing he was back there – that would be his worst nightmare – but of what it could have become. Were it still a live, thriving unit, pulsing with energy, forever ready to follow fresh artistic direction, had the relationships not broken down, he'd be there still, would have seen no reason ever to have left the 'best band in the world'. Andy will admit this without being pushed too hard. It doesn't ever dominate his day but you get the definite feeling that a little piece of his heart remains forever locked into that ideal, one that was briefly real.

As Rodgers and Kirke went on to a brief phase of gold- and platinum-glittered royalties and stadium sell-outs, Andy looked for a new musical existence. He had turned twenty a couple of weeks before he 'quit' the love of his life for the final time. What to do with the rest of it? Who was he when Free no longer existed? These were questions that would take literally decades to answer.

Just like last time we split, I went back to *Esgairs* and this time got really engrossed in writing new songs. It had now become even more a form of therapy, a necessity every day to express how I felt, kind of like the need to exercise, and I'd always feel better afterwards. I was quite happy just being where I was, taking a much needed break, drinking in life with a new perspective, finding my voice as a singer, and assessing the current reality.

I was invited to join The Faces as the bassist, but turned it down. We'd done a few tours with them and they had a very alcoholic, beery, 'lads' band' feel and that just wasn't me. Rod Stewart has a great way with an audience, getting everyone to join in – and he was like that in the bar at the hotel afterwards, 'Come on, come and have a drink' and not taking no for an answer. That was the whole culture of that band and it would have been a lot for me to cope with, totally outnumbered every night, down the bar, the one spoiling the party by not joining in. I don't think they were in the least interested in any aspect of me other than, 'You can play bass, you'll do,' which would be ignoring most of my personality. It wouldn't have been good. Rod is a great singer though. The Faces were messy but some of their stuff was pretty good. They ended up getting Tetsu from the latter days of Free – and predictably he ended up with a serious drink problem.

There was also some possibility of me working with Steve Winwood in a reformed Traffic. We jammed a little at his house but nothing became of that. He had moved from *The Cottage* – where the first Traffic album, which I love, had been created, a place in the middle of nowhere where you needed a Jeep to get to – to a full-on mansion, which I never got to see the full extent of, but was very beautiful, tastefully appointed, complete walls of record shelves. Blackwell used to park his Rolls-Royce there among the many others I saw. I always thought a Roller looked like a wedding cake on wheels. Driving around with Steve in his gold Lamborghini, I think he used to enjoy scaring the shit out of me; he'd pass a truck on a small country lane with another car coming the other way, knowing that he had the power and speed to do it. When he'd been in *The Cottage* I'd visited with my friend Albert, the crazy friend of the saxophonist from the old Lawless Breed days and who was now Steve's assistant and therefore at Island quite often and we'd hook up. He was still as crazy and loveable as ever and a bit of a druggie, though he always had it under control, unlike Koss who used it as an escape. The last time Albert had taken me down to Steve's place, Steve hadn't been there and, though I'm sure Steve would have killed him if he'd known, he'd played me what Steve was working on at the time, using a two-track Revox like we all did then; sounded great to me. Sadly Albert was killed in a car crash around this time.

I have great respect for Steve and he's a really nice guy too, but at the time he had me down there jamming it sort of felt like he didn't quite know what he wanted yet, and was trying out all kind of things, me among them. Plus I still wanted to find my own way too. The unit that he did form, with Rick Gretch I believe, seemed kind of directionless to me, so I wouldn't have fitted in. Also I think Winwood is by far a more mature musician than I, so it wouldn't have worked on many levels. His quiet, intense intelligence is also very intimidating.

Then this Canadian guy Marty Simon called out of the blue. He was a drummer and like most drummers, a very good talker. Got himself invited down in no time, and was behind the drum kit in my studio. He immediately showed himself to be a very talented drummer, very fluid, so we had an instant rapport. I had been quite happy just being where I was but Marty talked me around. Because a drummer has little value unless part of something else, they tend to be good at talking people into getting things together around them. Singers tend to think it's all about them but often it's initiated by the drummer. I have to take responsibility in allowing myself to just drift along with it. I should have been more firm about what I wanted. I was probably quite vulnerable, just hanging out, open to the universe, allowing any and all possibilities to present themselves, as one does when writing.

A guitarist became the first order of business, and it seemed like in no time we were around at Chris Spedding's place in Wimbledon, and there was no doubt he was a good guitarist. He was well thought of at the time, being a very in-demand studio player, like Jimmy Page, that could come in and do the job, no sweat. But he was kind of a fragile character. Interestingly, at that time Chris had never ever smoked a joint, which to me and Marty in those days seemed unusual. Because it was natural to just light one up, I watched Chris take his first toke, not knowing how later his drug indulgences would lead to heroin, again not unlike Jimmy Page.

The three of us rehearsed some of the new material I'd been writing and Island was fully supportive. Collectively, we were The Sharks. But, I don't know... it's almost as if I was on auto-pilot and the thing just took a life of its own and developed around me without me directing it, which was very remiss of me. In my mind, we were rehearsing the songs I'd written and would be singing. But somewhere along the line, either they or the label may have thought my singing wasn't strong enough and suddenly this guy 'Snips' [Steve Parsons] is in the picture as the singer. He had a gravelly voice, in the Joe Cocker mould, but it wasn't one I particularly liked. But I just sort of let it happen. Before I knew it, we were a band, press releases were going out saying 'Sharks: Andy Fraser's New Band' and I was answering reporters' questions as to when the record was being released, and tour dates etc. and the truth was Snips and myself were never on the same page. I was not continuing to work on my voice, but seemed to have got diverted, taken a major sideways turn.

Over the years, I have come to terms with the realisation that when one comes off a tour, it is not necessarily a bad thing to become a 'vegetable' for a while, which at first had me concerned. I now see that at times one gives out and at others you take in, and after a tour when you've given out so much, 'vegging out' is a reasonable way for the body to rebalance itself. So now I relax with it, and have come to expect it. I also suspect it makes one quite vulnerable before the process is completed.

First Water *was the name of The Sharks' album, recorded in December '72, released in April '73. Snips supplied four of the songs, Andy another four, with a further joint composition. It got good reviews but few sales. The songs were in the main catchy and raucous, rather in the vein of The Faces, without the subtlety of Free and rendered a difficult listen by Snips' voice, which sounds like a somewhat forced impersonation of Paul Rodgers or Rod Stewart but without the tone to carry it off. It seems a shame because Andy's voice, when it finally made a public airing a couple of years later on the first Andy Fraser Band album, was pretty damn good and certainly much more natural-sounding than Snips'.*

We toured and released the record but I just wasn't into it. This wasn't an acceptable situation. I'd been irresponsible in allowing it to happen, just going along with things. It was very out of character. It's all very well going with the flow but you've got to know when that's appropriate and when it's not, otherwise you can get yourself into a lot of trouble. I wasn't following my artistic instincts and felt trapped in a situation that fell far short of my expectations.

As soon as I came to this realisation, I felt I had to take responsibility and looked for a way out – which was triggered by a traffic accident on the way back from a gig. Blackwell had suggested we travel around in this swanky American car with a tail, teeth and fins on it, called 'The Sharkmobile' – very cheesy, I know, but they made it into a bit of a media thing. We were coming home one night, Spedding was driving and, being a bit dotty, he drove the fucking thing into a tree going round a roundabout, put a big V-shape into the front of the car. We'd only been going about 10mph, I've no idea how he lost control. I twisted my thumb pretty badly and was unable to play – and that created my out. I suggested they get another bass player and continue on. They did another record without me, then disbanded.

Chris Spedding went on to play with Paul McCartney, Snips did something with Ginger Baker. Marty? Well, he used to drive round in my car – the Mercedes I'd bought earlier – because I'd lost my licence, and he blew the engine one day and just abandoned it in Wimbledon somewhere, probably near Spedding's place. Then he went back to Canada. Last time I saw Chris he was in a junkie's hovel in California and my heart just cried. Again I felt helpless to do anything about it, just as with Koss, and although he wanted work, I just couldn't take that on. I've since heard he's doing much better, and hope it's true. He's basically a good guy, a very accomplished guitarist, and has really gone through it.

But one good thing came from Sharks. We'd been touring in Europe and were coming back to the UK on the ferry crossing from Calais to Dover when I met a striking Australian girl. I don't remember how we got talking, it was probably because she's a very outgoing, sociable person. She was welcome relief from the company of the Sharks and made that tiresome ferry ride a lot more bearable. Her name was Henrietta Shannon and she was backpacking her way around the world, an Aussie right of passage, it seems. She hadn't a clue who I was, and that always makes for a more real interaction, and had no other reason to want to be around me other than she liked my company.

She was an artist and had an adventurous, gypsy spirit, born and raised near Sydney, Australia on a large sheep farm. She'd trekked through Afghanistan – where she was given a black onyx ring by some big ol' hills man – then Turkey, where she had her passport and belongings stolen, then all across Europe. She was heading for England with no particular place to go. I suggested she come back to Surrey with me for a while, which she did – and never moved out. I abbreviated her name to 'Ri' – it was much easier to shout up the stairs than Henrietta – and we felt very easy in each other's company. After a couple of years she became pregnant with Hannah and we married. She gave me the onyx ring as my wedding ring.

I would describe our relationship as extremely positive. She is really smart, caring and very artistically creative. She is where our daughters Hannah and Jasmine get their artistic eye from. I would noodle around the studio writing songs, and she would paint or sketch, being what I consider to be on a par with Michelangelo. She would lightly draw circles on a page, stare at it then fill in body figures, and it was exactly like one of Michelangelo's pieces. There was a sense of calm productivity in the atmosphere which really encouraged creativity. I would say it was two artists in love. She would wander in and say, 'I like that sound,' and I would go check out what she was up to with her painting. Great days – idyllic.

On a side note, I also tend to see music and phrasing as circles, as opposed to linear lines. Imagine the many wheels on a clock, or the planets of a solar system, within a swirling galaxy; within a greater universe, circles within circles. I suspect the linear view is more of this world, and kind of like the flat earth theory. When I sing, my hands tend to start drawing circles, which is just the outer physical view of how I see the phrasing I am doing at the time. On camera it can look kinda funny, but that's what's going on. I find myself a better singer when my arms are free to swirl around, as opposed to being held down playing bass. I know people don't wanna hear that, want me forever to be the guy with the bass.

Ri opened my mind to a lot of new possibilities including, I must say, my first acid trip, which was a real changing point in my life. It lasted about three days, and went through stages of warm red, where everything I looked at was like for the first time, and I could appreciate its specialness, as though seeing things from a different planet – a great perspective. Alternatively, it would go to cold blue where I would shiver, and cry out to God. For most of the time I was running in and out of the studio playing music, holding a note on the piano, or just enjoying the timbre of my voice, saying, 'Ooh, aah, that sounds so good.' In fact I made some recordings and musical discoveries that prove it wasn't all in my head. It was a life-changing experience, which I have absolutely no misgivings about. Kind of like my world going from black and white, to vivid panoramic colour. It set a new bar – one which I had to learn how to match when not on acid.

In the middle of my noodling in the studio I got a call from Frankie Miller, completely out of the blue, this Glaswegian guy on the end of the phone telling me he was signed to Chrysalis. That was so characteristically him – he reached out to a lot of people out of the blue and went on to form great working relationships with them, people like Joe Walsh. He somehow just gets people involved, has that sociability about him. He'd also get so drunk he'd stand on your feet, no problem – but you don't mind.

I'm usually quite resistant to calls out of the blue; if someone calls me and I don't know them they've usually got about five seconds to identify themselves and give a good reason why they're interrupting me. He wanted to know if I'd be interested in writing stuff together and he just somehow got himself invited down, a bit like how Marty Simon had. We hit it off musically and personally, he is just a great guy – with a terrific voice. He became a very dear friend and was even best man at my wedding. I liked him so much I was prepared to put aside my own thing to help him in any way I could. I'm not sure if he had in mind to form a band, he was quite clever in being non-specific about that. At one stage we both went to see Chrysalis to discuss things and I was talking in terms of me and him and something about the reaction I got made me think, 'No, it's not you and Frankie, it's just Frankie.' That was just the vibe coming back and I hadn't even thought about it before. I was fine with that, I just gave myself to him, didn't ask anything in return. Joe Walsh later did the same for him. He had a way of making you feel like a really close friend, he was that sort of guy, very earthy and I don't recall him ever being down. I remember him falling asleep, but that doesn't count.

As well as writing stuff together I'd help him with the recording, play some bass, do some arranging. We were doing some stuff at the Island Basing Street studios once and Koss, who lived very near there, came along – and laid some guitar down. He played on 'I Know Why The Sun Don't Shine'. Koss was shit-faced but when he hit the notes they wailed! Some of his notes seemed to last five minutes, like he was in some parallel universe, but were interesting nevertheless, really crying out to you. He could still do it in spasms, but he was on that self-destructive slide to oblivion. Though we got some good stuff out of him at those recordings, I had the feeling he could be on another planet within the hour. At the time he lived in his mews house not far from the Basing Street studios, and I got the impression he would wind himself up all day, self-medicate, then go mooching around the studios, offering to play with whoever was there.

Frankie stayed at *Esgairs* quite a lot and he'd get hammered on booze until he was semi-conscious then I'd drag him up the stairs and put him to bed – which took some doing; he's a big heavy guy and tended to stomp on my feet during the effort. Ri and he got on really well too, he just became this lovely family friend. We worked on and off together for many years to come, though never as an official entity. He'd have the same way I had of creating something, which was to sing any kind of nonsense and listen to what kind of sounds were being made, then home in on it and scribble something down. But he was exhausting to work with, or even to keep company with. He'd use alcohol to open up and then coke to keep him going and we'd sit there and jam. There was always scotch and Coke and toot around with Frankie and you'd be rehearsing for a couple of hours and he'd say, 'Och, shall we take a ten-minute break down the pub,' – and that would be it, over for the day. I never liked pubs anyway, but this would signal that all creative energy was over. But even despite all that it was quite productive. In fact he even came over and stayed with me for a couple of weeks after I'd moved to the States and we wrote an album's-worth of material together then.

Frankie Miller had British chart success in 1975 with Andy's song 'Be Good To Yourself', originally written for the Free At Last *album but not included. Miller went on to a solid career as a performer, songwriter and actor before suffering a brain haemorrhage in 1994 while in New York. He was in a coma for three months and came out paralysed except for some arm movement. His brain is intact but wrapped in a body that doesn't function. He continues to make a slow recovery and can now walk and converse, completely confounding the doctors' predictions.*

He was very productive, always in a big hurry to do the next thing. Sometimes I wonder if there was something about his intuition where he knew he needed to do it real quick. We'll never know the answer to that. One of my fondest memories of Frankie is from my wedding day. It was a beautiful day as we walked out of the cottage that morning and Frankie had a bit of a hangover from the previous night. He said, 'Och, Andy, do ye really need te get married so early in the morning mahn? That sun is awfully bright, don't ye think?'

Ri and I had decided to marry when we were still in the maternity ward. I was with her during delivery as Hannah popped out and the attending nurse, in a very well rehearsed spiel, said, 'Right, what's the baby's last name?' She knew how to hit at exactly the right moment. Actually I understand that society has to have in place various protections for the children, and these protections come with marriage, as sanctioned by the state. In a lot of cases, I can see them being needed, when it comes to some deadbeat dads, but my responsibility has never come into question, so marriage was simply a formality.

Today, as gay couples are fighting for marriage rights, I have had to give the issue some thought. I have nothing against it, but it isn't an issue that is important enough for me to make a noise over, and I think that is because I personally don't need my relationships, gay or straight, to be sanctioned by church or state. They can both go to hell. I feel when people are hanging on to a religion that acts in such a homophobic, power-hungry, self-serving, manipulative way, they are having their true and earnest longings to be closer to God twisted and used by institutions that place themselves between you and God, deluding one into thinking, 'If you wanna get to God, you gotta go through them.' Bogus! I have no time for them, or a need for them to sanction my relationships.

One needs to separate God and Religion. God has always been. Religion is a bunch of institutions that have sprung up relatively recently in our planet's history and have nothing to do with the rest of the universe. In fact I feel it's much safer to be an atheist, which I am not, than to buy into the gobbledygook sold by the various religions. Until they can be separated, better to steer clear of it all, and some very intelligent people reason if God is about all this twaddle they read, then it's just myth. That's very sound logic until one separates God from the religion.

The wedding was a very perfunctory affair at the Woking register office. Before our few minutes with the registrar conducting affairs, we watched another couple through the waiting room windows get their photo taken, in full wedding dress, with the photographer – the only one in attendance – throwing confetti in the air just as he was snapping their picture. We all found this hilarious, and still hadn't quite gotten it under control when we were up next. I have memories of saying, 'Here, Ri, hold the baby while I try and find the ring. I'm sure I put it in one of my pockets.' Ah, so romantic.

Eventually Frankie went off to do his own thing and I started to regroup. I'd now built up a good collection of songs and effectively was starting again after the false start of Sharks, determined this time that I was going to perform them myself. I had a certain sound in my mind. I think I had visions of what synthesisers became and the kind of sounds you could get – but it was way too much hassle back then. You needed to be a computer nerd to get the sound you wanted, it just gave me a headache. But I was looking for that. When I heard Stevie Wonder and the sounds he was getting from Moog bass and keyboards I thought, 'Yeah, that's what I want.' Boy was he hot at that time. If The Beatles were in the moment for a few years then Stevie Wonder really captured that next moment.

I came across Nick Judd, a very good keyboard player. He'd been in the support band at a Sharks gig and had introduced himself then and he later played in Sharks after I'd left.

'It was at Leicester University, 1973,' recalls Judd. 'Sharks were touring to promote the First Water *album. I remember when we played Andy and Steve were watching from the side. I also remember charging into their dressing room in an inebriated state and I started waffling about what a terrific set they had played – which they had – but I didn't think they were too happy. I got the call to join a few weeks later, by which time Andy had moved on.'*

We hooked up and he was unusual in that he was playing bass pedals, which allowed me to play this weird sort of fuzzy lead bass and I reckoned with that combination and the sort of sound I was after we didn't really need a guitarist. Besides, I was sort of wary of guitarists by this point, seeing them as potential trouble. For a drummer we hooked up with Kim Turner, a very young kid with hardly any experience but a ton of infectious, positive, motivating energy, which I loved. His brother had been in Wishbone Ash and through them was connected to their manager Miles Copeland.

After our time together Kim had gone to Miles, still a teenager, looking for a job and just worked as a general dogsbody in the office then progressed from there. When he first started rehearsing with us, he needed bus fare money!

Many years later he went on to co-manage The Police with Miles and would also manage me in the '80s, by which time he was driving round in the latest model Mercedes. He was a great, very generous guy, very open and likeable. Sadly he died of cancer a couple of years ago.

The Andy Fraser Band was the name of the eponymous album, released in 1975 by CBS, Andy's first non-Island venture in the UK. It's a nice piece of work, Andy's voice is revealed as toneful though at this stage still very much in the Free mould. The songs are strong, the sound, with the gurgling pedals, fuzzy bass and absence of guitar is distinctive, but with hindsight it's a transitional record, a document of Andy feeling his way as a solo artist, the songs not yet distanced far enough from the style of Free but without that band's oomph and power. 'Ain't Gonna Worry' and 'Keep On Loving You' are the two stand-out tracks, soulful rockers both.

He was a restless artist at this time, still searching, as was evidenced when he disbanded that group almost immediately and recorded an album – In Your Eyes – in the legendary Muscle Shoals studio in Birmingham, Alabama – with some of the studio's top session musicians. This was much more of an R&B-style of music, with extensive brass and backing vocals, though the Free At Last *-overspill song 'Be Good To Yourself' is more in keeping with the rockier feel of the previous album, if not as raucous as Frankie Miller's hit-single version. Despite being surrounded by a totally different group of musicians,* In Your Eyes *was still billed as The Andy Fraser Band, indicating perhaps that he was officially beginning to cut the apron strings that had always made him a member of a band. The word 'band' may have been in the title, but realistically Andy was essentially now a solo artist. The only band he'd ever been comfortable in was long-gone.*

In Your Eyes came about purely from the sudden availability of Muscle Shoals and the associated musicians. I had a drunk Welshman, Corridick Davis, for a manager at this time and he'd somehow managed to swing it that I could go out there. But it was a mismatch in that these people were way superior to me as a singer. They were used to making records with people like Aretha Franklin and it would have taken someone of that calibre to handle the schedule of slamming down ten tracks in five days, do the vocals on the sixth day and mix on the seventh – because that was all the time that was available. My inexperienced voice made them sound way more slick and it needed a more experienced vocalist to bring it more in perspective. Alabama was a weird place at the time in that it was a dry state, no alcohol allowed. They had a secret stash downstairs in the studio but on weekends everybody would drive over the border and get shit-faced because it was legal there.

It was now the mid-70s and it had probably been too long since Free for Andy to have used the momentum of the band to become established as a solo artist. His projects were stop-start, still searching for the elusive magic ingredient. Toby, Sharks, working with Frankie Miller, meeting Ri, discovering acid, two versions of an Andy Fraser Band: all these things used up time, a period long enough for him to have become almost forgotten by the public at large. There's also the sense that no matter how good his musical endeavours might be, they weren't Free; that magical partnership before the dynamics got screwed up just couldn't be repeated. He was searching for new direction, tentatively pushing, but something wasn't working. That restlessness was a symptom of something undefined, something not being fulfilled. A letter from the tax man triggered the beginning of a resolution.

For the first eight years of being a working individual I had never paid any taxes because usually you get a national insurance number and I never had one – and I just thought, 'When they send the tax bill I'll pay it.' It took them eight years and I hadn't kept any records so they pulled this number out of the air, interest and penalties and said, 'Pay this.' It was a ludicrous amount and together with the cold weather, my mum's death and people OD-ing around me, it led to the idea of getting the hell out of Britain and getting a little bit of Californian sunshine. Being sponsored by Island's American department meant I was able to get a green card. They claimed that as a songwriter I was unique and my work couldn't be replicated by an American. The fact that I was earning good money helped.

Ri agreed it was a good idea and the plan was that I would go over there and find a place to buy while she stayed in the UK and looked after the selling of the cottage. We were going to start a new life.

They were. But it wasn't going to be anything like the one they pictured.

ALL RIGHT NOW

May 7, 1976. It's one of the few dates I remember. That's when I finally officially moved to the USA. California sunshine, a completely new chapter, a different planet almost, it felt incredibly liberating, leaving a lot of baggage behind in the rain of England.

A couple of months earlier, while checking out California property, Andy had received the news he'd been expecting for some time: Paul Kossoff was dead. Gone, just eight years after the pair of teenagers jammed together for the first time at Andy's mum's house, through superstardom and break-up and drugs hell – an accelerated lifetime for a beautiful but tragically fragile soul, now free at last. An empty, used body crumpled in the locked toilet of an airplane, no-one even aware he was gone until the time came to prepare for landing and he wasn't in his seat. Gone to some higher place where the physical torments were over. He'd been here and he made his beautiful mark on the world, one that can forever be heard, in a life that seemed barely any longer than a gorgeously sustained wail of his Les Paul.

I heard he'd died on a plane. It sort of hit me like I knew this was coming and now it's come today. It wasn't a surprise. Like I said, it was a slow suicide and had been unfolding towards its inevitable conclusion. I guess the fact that it's today rather than yesterday or tomorrow grabs you by the collar a bit but it was so obviously coming. He couldn't – wouldn't – be helped. He'd worked since the demise of Free because there were always people seeking him out, saying you need to do something here. But it was really all just going on around him; I don't think he ever thought, 'OK, I need to make a fresh start here.' He was on the long downwards slide to oblivion and there was no pulling him back.

I was shocked to then receive a letter from his father David, in which he blamed me for his son's death. I had no idea whether the others received a similar letter or whether he targeted only me until fairly recently after noting it on my website bio. Others, even non-band members, said the same thing. David Kossoff denied it right up until he was on his deathbed, and then I heard from David Clayton, author of the Free book, that he finally came clean. I understood he was grieving and I didn't respond, neither did I attend the funeral, mainly because it was arranged by his family and I wasn't invited. One doesn't gate-crash a funeral, which is essentially for the grieving family, and they obviously preferred me not to be there. In a sense, I'd already done my grieving for Koss. It was a done deal he was going and it was incredibly sad but I'd already moved on when the official news came.

It may sound callous, down there in black and white on the page, but it's not. Andy had lost Koss already – when he'd refused the kidnapping rescue. He was already on the road to 'that stupid club' as Kurt Cobain's mother would later term the prematurely dead rock star roll-call. Andy had then lost even the sad walking shadow of the old, funny, vibrant Koss when Free fell apart the second time, just like he'd lost the Paul Rodgers he'd known and loved, subsumed by a different man that looked and sounded the same but wasn't. That was all gone – and hanging around in England, moving in the same musical and social circles as before, seeing the same scenery, was maybe part of why Andy felt it was time to try a different movie, a new one that wasn't the sad post-script to some old blockbuster. Nothing left to keep him in England, after all.

At the risk of amateur psychology, you might wonder too if there was not something wilful within Andy's sub-conscious behind the decision to make the move. Whether he knew it or not, was there not a gay man inside there, silently screaming – at the conventional marriage and life he'd found himself in? Seen from that perspective, moving to a different country was a rejection of his history, a fresh-start, a situation much more conducive to being able to come out.

Probably something in that. There was a lot of repression going on. The move to the States was a big thing, and with hindsight the first stage in letting everything go. But the circumstances of my separation from Ri really accelerated the whole thing. She was supposed to be following me across one month later. That one month became six – during which time I had my first gay encounter.

I'd gone down to the beach in Malibu. It wasn't a gay beach as far as I knew but I started talking to this guy. He was making all the moves and it took me a while to catch on, but once I did I found myself not at all averse to the idea. I'd been apart from Ri long enough to be a bit sexually frustrated but without my realising it, the thought of sex with females had diminished. This guy was about my age, very friendly and good-looking. He asked me back to his house nearby and my mind was reeling with the possibilities. It turned out he had just broken up with the actor Richard Chamberlain – there were pictures of them together all over the house. He was a great host and we enjoyed the afternoon. It was very casual, but the first thing you could call a gay experience. We never met again and he didn't jump out to me as 'the guy to be in my life' – it was way too early to be thinking like that, but what was remarkable afterwards was the feeling that I had somehow 'found home', not with the guy but with the act. However I then again went into deep denial – even though it had just happened! I began to treat it as if it had been just an aberration. I re-compartmentalised it all. There was a lot of digesting and assimilating – and maybe repression – going on, a very strange and powerful denial.

The delay of Ri and Hannah joining me in the States definitely played its part in that first little adventure. The reason for that delay was only partly to do with her not being able to sell the house in England. She had also become friendly with some devotees of the Indian guru Baba Muktananda and had become a disciple herself. She'd visited his ashrams and become completely influenced by the whole thing. By the time she finally joined me in the States, I hardly knew her. She'd become a strict vegetarian, had foresworn any recreational drug intake, chanted Hare Krishna from four in the morning and critically, there was no sex or music. The guru had said these things were just distractions from the real purpose of life, indulgences. In her new lifestyle *everything* was out – except her devotion to this guru.

I think I'm an open-minded person and I tried to accept this new Ri and her radically changed views. I read all the literature, visited ashrams here, there and everywhere, meditated with her and really gave it a go.

We hadn't sold the house in England and instead we rented it out to this band, Rough Diamond, that was contracted to Island.

Rough Diamond was a prog-flavoured rock band formed by ex-Uriah Heep member David Byron and Clem Clempson, guitarist from Humble Pie. The line-up was completed by former Wings drummer Geoff Britton. They released one record, in 1977, to lukewarm reviews and few sales. With the punk movement now in full flow, it was a bad time to be a prog-rock band.

They were a bunch of smack-heads who never paid one cent of rent and trashed the place, literally ripped out toilets and sinks and threw them outside, just in some kind of drugged stupor, I guess. They also graffiti-ed the house. There was a story that they were coming through customs one day and their manager got busted with smack on him and he ratted on his wife in trying to get out of it. That's the kind of people they were. Old English law didn't allow me to just throw them out. I literally had to pay them to leave. It was a very painful lesson. But even with the house in the state it was, I still managed to sell it eventually for a profit that was literally just under ten times what I'd paid for it.

I was continuing to write and play music. In fact it's one thing I've never stopped doing, even when I wasn't releasing anything. I've got shelves full of stuff and if you hear it all in chronological order you can hear the progression through the years; it all makes sense.

It's true. I've been privileged to hear quite a lot of it. There are masses of CDs and sound files of unreleased material, some of it just in basic demo form, other songs with full production applied – and when your hear them it's easy to pretty much define the vintage immediately. First of all there's the development of his voice, moving away from the Free-style rock belter to a more sophisticated and natural tone, warmer, not stretching so hard. Later still, its natural scale moves down an octave or so, giving it the authority of hard-won experience. There's a much more obvious relationship between his speaking voice and singing voice than with most singers. Then there's the way the sound is always absolutely of that moment: 1976 has the aesthetic of Songs In The Key Of Life -era Stevie Wonder, 1984 is full-on 80s glitz and harsh colours, more recent stuff has the incredible combination of fidelity and power that current technology provides.

By the time I got to the States I was moving away from rock music towards a more soulful direction. I'd taken a drummer with me from England, a guy called Tony Hicks from the jazz-rock band Back Door. He brought his wife and new baby over and we all lived in this huge house I'd rented in Brentwood in the Santa Monica mountains overlooking LA. So it felt like quite a weight I was carrying. The living room was large enough to set up band equipment and we began trying out musicians there.

Tony Hicks was a big character from Middlesbrough, had probably seen Free in their pomp at Redcar and was yet another close associate of Alexis Korner. He died in 2006 but three years earlier gave an interview to the Cultural Foundation website. His take on his period with Andy is an interesting one: '[Andy] wanted to be Stevie Wonder. He's a beautiful songwriter, tremendous... but the record company wanted him to be Paul Rodgers because Bad Company had become so big. So it was a drama, forever arguing, New York on the phone, but it was great fun recording with him.'

I found other musicians over here. The attitude of musicians over here was completely different to that in the UK, where everyone just pitched in and there was a real sense of camaraderie. Here, the musicians are divided into the main guy and the support players. The main guy does the writing, gets the deals, hires the studio and hires the musicians, who want to know how much they will be paid to rehearse. It took a while to wrap my head around that but it was the first step in growing stronger and taking more responsibility, becoming more of a complete individual. You suddenly realise it's all on you. That's a big one to get in front of.

We recorded an album for Polydor as The Stealers. It included 'Every Kinda People' and a bunch of other really strong songs. They took a listen to it and said, 'We need to get our A&R guy to remix this.' They did that and I listened to it and was appalled. It sounded so weak and wanky and I said, 'No way are you putting this out.' So that was the end of that relationship. The record just stayed on the shelf, though later Robert Palmer had quite a big hit with 'Every Kinda People'.

Palmer did indeed score well with that particular song of Andy's, the record reaching number 16 in the US billboard in 1978 and playing a big part in establishing Palmer as a major solo artist. He and Andy went back a long way and remained firm friends until Palmer's sudden death in 2003 but the bringing together of Palmer and the song had nothing to do with their friendship; it was initiated by Island – to whom Andy was still contracted as a writer – picking it as a suitable number for the laid-back classy style they were trying to project for the crooner. It's a gorgeous song, simple and powerfully soulful in both its lyrics and sound, the dreamy opening refrain drilling itself into your head for days, the busy rumbling bass diving this way and that over the relaxed melody of the verses like a babbling brook over a rock, before the song soars free for the chorus. It's the greatest song Marvin Gaye never wrote and most songwriters would give their right arm to have come up with just this one perfect number. By rights it should put Andy in the pantheon of songwriting greats. In style, it's a million miles from Free and offers some clue to the places Andy was reaching for, the aspirations he had for that band. The thought of an evolved Free – one that had stayed together and embraced Andy's vision - performing this belongs to some perfect other universe.

Back in this universe, the song's quality just makes the shelving of The Stealers album from which it came seem a real shame. Other songs from that album were subsequently recorded by Joe Cocker ('Loving You' and 'Sweet Little Woman', a version of the latter also recorded by Lulu as 'Sweet Little Darlin'').

Robert was the loveliest guy. He used to come and watch us when Free used to play this small club in Scarborough. He used to say he always thought of himself as a bass player's singer and that he used to come to watch us for the bass. I'd always assumed he'd be more focussed on Paul. At some point in his life he'd decided 'drugs are for me' and he had quite a substance problem as well as being an alcoholic – he'd have gin for breakfast. In some of his later videos you can just about see the bloat behind the suave suits. He was such a good looking guy when he was young though, exceptional. Sometimes he'd phone, him and his wife both out of it, and they'd just talk over each other to you for an hour or two! I could put the phone down and go make a sandwich, come back and they'd still be talking! He'd be in a coke-infused alcoholic stupor and you didn't really need to answer him. When he became successful he lived in this beautiful converted mill in Switzerland with a lake view, which was great to see. He had a car on permanent call in case he wanted to go to the shop or something. He never did learn to drive. A warm, wonderful, generous-spirited man.

It's interesting to speculate on whether 'Every Kinda People' would have broken Andy through as a major solo star had his version been released as a single and received appropriate promotional back up. As it was, he remained out of public view.

Things weren't going well with Ri who continued to be totally devoted to the guru. 'Baba said music is an addiction that needs to be cured,' was one of the things she said and I'm like, 'Oh, fuck!' at this point. We did somehow manage to conceive another child – Jasmine – during this time. Ri decided that it had been decreed by Baba, or he played some part other than how babies usually come into being. We were on totally different pages. Incidentally, Jasmine's middle name is Mukti after Muktananda. We all went over to India a few times – I gave it every opportunity. If there was something in this I wanted to find out what it was. But ultimately, it seemed like more organised religion bullshit – and it even had me doubting God for a time. These devotees would go over there, pay rent to stay there and then spend their time building him new apartments, making him fabulously wealthy! I remember going to pay the rent when I was there and the books being open I saw a whole lot of fuckin' zeros after the numbers and I thought, 'What a scam this is.'

Swami Muktananda died in 1982, since which time various unflattering stories have emerged about him. Andy's financial assessment was apparently spot-on, if the guru's frequent sightings walking between Lear Jet and waiting limo are any guide – all paid for by the labours and payment of his followers. There are also stories that far from 'practising what he preached' regarding the foregoing of sex – he was in fact, it seems, very active in that department, particularly with chosen young female disciples, if their testimonies are to be believed. Maybe the 'universal' rules didn't apply to him. Sounds like the guy lived more of a rock star's life than Andy...

Ri and I kept trying to make it work for a few years and in terms of spending time with the girls, seeing them develop, it was great. I like to think I was quite hands-on. I have memories of nappy-changing and later preparing meals for them because like all kids they want French fries and you're trying to get vegetables in them. I'd make a salad and cut it up to form smiley faces, with cherry tomatoes for the eyes, cucumber for the nose, broccoli for the hair and they'd giggle and giggle.

Hannah was and is the more outgoing of the two. She was initially very shy, used to hide behind her mother's skirt, but there was one plane journey where something in her just seemed to click and she was running up and down the aisle, talking to everybody. She's been like that ever since! She's also quite the hustler – and that's something I recognise from myself, especially when I was younger – and not afraid of hard work. Jasmine appears more demure although when it comes to it she's a rock in the road. I also see that in me at other times. Once she's decided something you cannot move her. In her way she's stronger than all of us, though very quiet. They're both very creative and very beautiful.

Ri would spend a lot of time with the girls in India, leaving me to my own devices in California. With no sex, the urges came upon me – and they definitely weren't for women any longer. So that's when I began taking my first gay baby steps. It was trial and error at first – and completely terrifying. I went to Hollywood thinking the gay bars have got to be around here somewhere, I'd talk to someone on the street who looked kind of gay, try to get some clues. It took a really long time for me to figure it out where these places were.

Eventually I found this placed called Rage in West Hollywood, which was quite a popular spot. I'd been pointed there by a couple of gay hustlers. They seemed like nice enough guys actually and I wasn't so much looking for sex from them – though we did have sex – as information about the gay scene. My main memory of Rage is one of panic in between getting out the car and walking into the bar – about being recognised. There were two different worlds I was trying to bridge here and they were not meeting. I had images of being spotted and outed. I couldn't even be out to myself yet, so being out to anyone else seemed inconceivable. I walked in there, adrenaline pumping, trying to look cool and calm.

It was all pretty casual inside. There was a cafe and out back a dance place, with music blaring. I went back there a few times. It took some time to decode it all. Sometimes the less you say the more you're liked and it's often done with eye contact, all sorts of stuff I'm not particularly comfortable with as I like to be open and free with people. But anyway, I gradually made progress, found my way around – and had plenty of opportunity to do so with Ri away so much.

One time I was in there and recognised the singer from a British northern band and I went up to him and introduced myself. He must have been at an even earlier stage of denial than me because at the first opportunity he was out of there – didn't see him for dust – and it was only a few years later he came out.

In between times I'd be wrestling with myself internally: I couldn't be gay – yet I clearly was. Then I must cure myself and I'd try to do that, then it would happen again. There was also the guilt about doing this behind Ri's back. This went on for years. My career seemed to be on the backburner, I guess because this was my big issue now. I was still writing and recording at home but the idea of performing didn't sit at all comfortably with me anymore. You need to be comfortable with yourself before you can possibly get on a stage and let yourself be seen by thousands of eyes. I was still reaching for a place I felt far away from. How could I project myself if I wasn't even comfortable with who I was? If you're uncomfortable with yourself it's going to be hell. It's hard for anyone to come out, even if you're an office worker. But being in the public eye as well just makes it look like a mountain.

It was surely the stuff of sweaty nightmares. Try to put yourself there. All those eyes staring at you, trying to see through you, maybe seeing a part of you withheld even from yourself – caught! A raving queer! Fears of a broken family, a ruined career, the violent ripping apart of the picture you were trying to hold onto of yourself. In the paranoia your angst created, maybe you'd worry that you wouldn't quite carry off a gesture, unable to convincingly transmit that self-image you were struggling to hold onto internally – and they'd be upon you, tearing you to shreds. And how do you hold onto a pole made ever more slippery by the sweat of those fevered nightmares? The inevitable was surely coming... just a matter of time. The sharks were circling, thousands of them, down there in the blackness beyond the edge of the stage. All those eyes. Watching.

Can you imagine anything more difficult within this struggle than trying to make the transition in your career from band member to front man? Of all the things you wouldn't want to be trying to accomplish as you went through the process of coming out... Little wonder things were about to come grinding to a halt. Meantime Andy's management was pushing for a record. It had been several years since the stillborn Stealers.

By this time my former drummer Kim Turner was acting as my manager. Back then, I'd given him bus fare money to get to rehearsals. Now he was vastly successful as co-manager of The Police. He was such a positive force – and it was Kim that really pushed me into getting something together. I'd decided this time that I wasn't going to play bass, that I wanted to concentrate fully on my singing. It's not a natural combination anyway – as a bassist you need to be behind the beat, as a singer just ahead of it. I'm a different person as a singer than when I'm a bass player. On the bass my hands are moving slowly whereas as a singer you're in double time, ahead of the rhythm. If you're too in tune with the rhythm you sound like a drum machine; you need to be ahead of it like a master of ceremonies, using the right side of the brain. Besides, you only have so much to give as a performer and this was splitting it in two. I'd built up a good collection of songs and I began pulling a band together to rehearse at the studio in Tujunga. Again, I had to pay them.

I got a guy called Michael Thompson on guitar – a hell of a player – and Bob Marlette, who was not only an extremely talented keyboard player but also had good songwriting ideas too and we wrote some stuff together. On bass was Davey Faragher, who has been with Elvis Costello ever since and on drums Tony Braunagel, who'd been a house drummer with Island and had worked in the past with Koss and later went on to play with Bonnie Raitt and Robert Kray. We rehearsed for months and months. They'd all come up to my house in

Tujunga on a ridge that jutted out and on one side was the whole valley and on the other national forest. I had one of the roads leading off past a horse corral into a fire trail; I'd go running there in the morning. The studio was a converted stables, about 70 feet long, kinda thin. You could look out both sides – one to the city, one to the wilderness. It was a fantastic place, I loved it.

Suddenly one day a male peacock just arrived there and hung around. No explanation. I left bird food around, and outside one of the windows of the studio was an eighteen-inch-high rock with a scooped out top, which I would fill with water every day, to encourage it to hang around. Funny bird. It would lie alongside the long glass sliding door, with mega decibels of music blaring out, and seem to quite like it. When I would wander back to the house, it would follow me like a dog, but if I turned around it would pretend to be busy checking out the flowers or something, never really acknowledging me. One day it just disappeared, looking for a mate maybe.

Ri and the girls were in India again and so I was full-on into the recording. In the middle of all this I decided to come clean to Ri. I phoned her in India and told her everything; that I was gay, that I'd had homosexual experiences while she'd been away. I was somewhat surprised by the way it didn't seem to resonate with her at all. She didn't verbalise it quite like this, but the vibe was very much along the lines of, 'Oh well, we're not having sex now anyway because I'm a spiritual person.' We must have been deluded because we then agreed that for the sake of the girls we would still live together. Ri ended up moving into the guest house we had, but it was incredibly tense and after a few months it was very obvious to both of us that it just wasn't working – and couldn't ever work. Thinking back, I've really no idea how we ever thought that arrangement could possibly work. It was such a weird time.

With the recording finished, I presented it to Island and Blackwell came back and said, 'Well, we'd like to sign you but not the band.' That came as a bolt out of the blue for me; I'd been thinking of them as band members, which actually doesn't compute given that I was paying them just to rehearse. But it knocked the life out of the unit. Michael Thompson said, 'I'm out of here,' and went on to play with the likes of Mariah Carey and Celine Dion and we toured the record without him. It was a joyless tour. On top of my own discomfort about performing there was not a good vibe in the band, as you can imagine. Aside from the fact that they hadn't been signed, Bob Marlette was a difficult character to have on the road. His attitude had the other guys saying to me, 'You've got to do something about Bob.' It didn't help that he was hugely overweight and just not suited to being on a gruelling tour schedule. It made for a bad atmosphere.

The original idea was to have the title track as the single but then at the last minute Blackwell said, 'Do you know what would be a great idea? If you did a cover of 'Do You Love Me?',' and I said, 'OK.' But it was so the wrong direction. It was trying to make a Michael Jackson out of me, which I so clearly wasn't. For the first time I did a video – as this had become an essential thing if the song was going to get any airplay. Throwing a musician into what is essentially acting, an entirely new discipline, isn't to be taken lightly. Your musical abilities count for nothing and it becomes all about how you interact with the camera. The video was awful. I really tried and just crippled myself. It was a stupid idea and really just a death knell to the whole project.

The spectacle of a white disco-suited Andy dancing and miming to his recording of the old cheesy Berry Gordy-written number in a cringe-worthy bar-room scene, knee skids, open arms and acrobatics, makes you doubt what your eyes are telling you: he looks like Andy Fraser, the cool and very measured guy from Free, but surely he can't be. It was 1984 and given that this was the first time anything had been publically released by him in almost a decade, he still looked great. He could've passed for twenty-one – he was in fact thirty-one - and was clearly full of energy. But there's no way around it: it was a god-awful spectacle and really wasn't him. Given what we now know about his personal struggle behind the scenes, you have to admire his sheer commitment to the task in hand – but what a horribly ill-considered task. It smacks of Blackwell giving only cursory thought to the matter: 'What's the in style at the moment? Michael Jackson-style dance videos. Let's get Andy to do that. Think of an up-tempo number, get him to do a cover of it. That should work on MTV.' It was surely suggested with Andy's best interests at heart, trying finally to break him out as a major solo act in the prevailing fashion of the time, but took precious little account of his character and none at all of his musical progression from Free onwards.

That said, it's impossible trying to second-guess where an artist wants to go – and in Andy's case there were few clues from the outside. His previous commercial success had allowed him the luxury of big gaps in his recorded output and during this time, as fashions changed, it meant only he could know what his true musical north was. We could see he'd left behind straight-ahead rock 'n' roll, had shown some inclination towards blue-eyed soul, had written a beautiful example of the genre in 'Every Kinda People', but now was apparently into middle-ground 'AOR' if the songs on Fine Fine Line *are any guide. The songs are polished, professional and of the time, not a million miles away from the sort of stuff that had re-birthed Steve Winwood as a major artist of the '80s. But they're largely generic in their lyrical content and it doesn't take a genius to work out that his struggles with his own identity – and his resistance to what in hindsight was obvious – limited not only the drive but also the direction of his career. He needed to be comfortable with what he was presenting to the world and on this record he's not sticking his neck out at all. It's very... safe; maybe his last serious attempt at something consciously commercial.*

Four-on-the-floor rock is an unsuitable framework for a gay guy to work within. That may sound like a generalisation, but really its transcendental moments are invariably the stuff of boy-girl adolescence and the thrills therein. This wasn't Andy, though he'd been a driving force in one of the greatest of such bands. His shift away from that as his musical palette changed is understandable, but the internal battle that so slowed his coming out to himself evidently had the same effect on his career trajectory – even though he was creating music virtually throughout.

A defining moment came in the immediate aftermath of a gig on the Fine Fine Line *tour. A female fan had somehow cajoled her way back stage, intent on 'bagging' Andy.*

I thought, 'Why not?' and we were having sex when at some point I just thought, 'You know, I'm not really into this. It's just not doing it for me.' That was the last time I had heterosexual sex.

Not long after the tour ended, Ri and I had to admit that the idea of us trying to live together just couldn't work. We needed to be realistic. As divorces go, it was as good as it could be. She told me what she needed , it was reasonable and I gave it to her without any kind of argument. That was that. I always sent money for the kids for as long as they needed it and there were never any squabbles. It was obviously better that she had the kids rather than me, while I tried to sort out my life. The girls couldn't have had a better mother, and Ri is to be credited with how wonderfully well they've turned out. But psychologically it wasn't easy for either of us. Coming to terms with being gay took me well over a decade from that first encounter, and Ri went through traumatic times, feeling she was to blame for me 'turning gay' – something that's apparently not too uncommon in these situations.

My whole world had fallen apart. At Ri's suggestion in the immediate aftermath of breaking up I went to see a counsellor. It was so pathetic! I told him my story and he started crying! I'm paying him to sit there crying like a baby! I thought, 'I don't want to do this more than once,' and didn't go back. I got better counselling from the street subsequently.

My marriage was over, my latest musical project had died a death. It was time to just let everything go. I'd never done anything else in my life than be a musician and I'm sure certain aspects of me were retarded, including sexually. I didn't have a normal teenager experience, no hanging round in bars, no experimenting. Then I'd been locked into a marriage with kids. Suddenly that was all gone and the only thing to do was fall over the cliff and let go of it all – everything: career, marriage, the picture I'd presented to the outside world. It was time to really find myself.

ALL RIGHT NOW

The house was kinda empty without them – and even though I was used to that as they'd been away so much, it was the beginning of a very different time for me. For maybe the first time in my life I sat still. I hadn't realised how locked into myself I'd become. I'd always busied myself so much I never allowed myself to think about it, but the penny was beginning to drop within me – in between the conflicts.

About the only person I had regular contact with at this time was my faithful gardener, a very humble, hardworking and ethical guy – reminded me of Jesus, in fact! He had a real pureness about him and everyone really liked him. Every now and then he'd bring someone round to help out and one day I got talking with this guy he'd brought who told me about this book I might want to check out, called *The Urantia Book*. He came and went out of my life and had no other meaning to me than that brief exchange. I can't even remember his name, but he changed my life, my whole perspective on life.

Stand by for a spiritual digression. The Urantia Book *is a tome – supposedly created by the transcribing of the trance-like speech of a Chicago man for a period of years during the 1920s – claiming to be a channelling from higher beings of the true nature of the universe, a supposed explanation of the source material from which all man-made religions have been formed. Quite a leap of faith...*

Yeah, I hesitate to talk about it. But it's sort of like the Bible; includes it, explains it, takes it out of the 'Sunday school' level, corrects misconceptions. It's not trying to sell you a religion; in fact it frowns upon that. They don't want to know who you are, the book is there available for you to buy or download but they don't want to know anything about you, don't try to sell you anything else. But I found the contents quite mind-blowing and it has moved me. It's incredibly dense and for a whole year after Ri and I split I would set aside time each day after exercising to read and try to understand this book. It took me a year to get through it, reading it pretty much every day for an extended period and I've just let it filter through over the years. I've no interest in trying to convert anyone to it, but nothing I've ever read has made more sense.

It helped me during my struggle. There were times when I was contemplating suicide, as the idea of being gay still refused to resolve itself within me. There were many tortured nights of the soul. I read a book by an NBC reporter who had helped her sick mother die a humane death and she explained how you went about getting the right combination of medications necessary by telling one doctor you had this problem, another one you had a different problem and so on until you had the right combination to painlessly do the job. I got all my affairs in order, looking to make it as easy and tidy as possible for everyone afterwards. It got to the stage where in my mind the deed had already happened – and then I thought about it from that perspective, thinking, 'What the hell did that solve?' The answer was nothing. That was a crucial stage of acceptance. I still had a vast way to go, but I'd dismissed the easy, pointless way out. We're sent here to make a contribution and to get over our hurdles, whatever they may be – so I just had to get on with doing that, no matter how un-jumpable that hurdle appeared to be.

The Urantia Book helped make sense of it. It made me resolve how could I be one of God's soldiers if I couldn't even accept myself? I found God when I found I was gay. I finally got perspective on this little speck in the vast universe. My experiences of letting go of everything during this time – image, career, marriage – stripped everything back to reveal all that was left. It took a while, a number of years, it didn't just happen during this time. But this was definitely a breakthrough for me, when the pieces began to fall into place.

Both processes progressed on parallel tracks and I'm sure that's not a coincidence. Both were internal things. As far as I can see God has got nothing to do with organised religions. You're searching for God and these religious people are pointing you in the wrong direction. People have bought into the scam that if you want to get to God you've got to go through these religions. To commune with God is to go inward and when you confess to an outer party, it's completely the wrong direction. I'm not sure if it's evil or merely ignorant but it's definitely wrong. Saying that out loud is like swearing at the Pope which definitely didn't do Sinead O'Connor any good.

Similarly, being gay was just about me. I didn't – and still don't – feel part of any gay 'community'. Gay entertainment, drag shows and stuff, just don't do it for me. I'm speculating these things are a form of rebellion internalised in a negative way. I don't relate to the camp way a lot of gay guys are with each other, just like I don't identify with hetero guys who sit and talk about sports with each other. I don't feel like I'm in either camp, I'm just me – and it would be great if everyone could just get past the gay/straight thing. I'd love that distinction to just disappear. For the younger generations I think that's happened or is happening.

My intake of acid probably helped me during this time. If possible I would have taken it every day, but you actually can't. It doesn't work because your body gets used to it. You have to build up your vitamins and minerals again because acid quickly depletes them. But for me an acid trip was the most pure sense of being, seeing beauty in everything and wanting for nothing. A sip of water would be incredibly satisfying, the sound of your voice, everything you look at – and there was something about it that made you physically feel very lithe. I can't do it now because of my enforced health regime but if it wasn't for that I'd still do it. One can't develop anything like a physical addiction to it; physiological I suppose, like food with some people. It was just nice and you always want more candy, but that doesn't mean you can't do without candy. I had to learn how to perform at the same level without it, so it set a very high bench mark.

After about a year living there on my own, finally it was time to leave Tujunga. I did a very uncharacteristically carefree thing: I thought, 'Let's get out there and muck about, just indulge myself.' It was part of the act of letting go, probably the definitive part. I sold up and bought a motorhome and had it kitted out with a studio and solar panels that charged the batteries, had a motorbike on the back. It was very cool.

At first I had some idea about going down to Mexico in it, then I discovered they didn't have cash dispensers down there – and I thought, 'Screw that!' Instead I just drove anywhere the fancy took me. I didn't even have a map. I just set off on the road and stayed on it for about the next two years. I would just drive into a town, find somewhere nice to stop – by a lake or something – and just stay there. Of course, having your own hotel on wheels meant I could also just pull up somewhere near any gay bars and not have to worry about how I was getting home. I was getting bolder with experimenting, feeling that if I drove into some anonymous town and found a gay bar I could just go in there and no-one would even know who I was, whereas if I tried to do that in Hollywood I was terrified – an unbelievable head trip just getting from the car to the bar.

It was a really fun time, albeit maybe slightly unreal in that I didn't have a budget concern. It being the '80s I was starting to get into coke around this time, before it got boring. I'd drive along, have a bit of a tune, get high. Obviously there's a danger with any kind of indulgence, and it hit home to me in the aftermath of a particular night. I'd gone into this bar and I was never a big drinker but someone had got me loaded very early with tons of shots. Within half an hour I was blotto. I went to the motorhome with this guy and we decided to drive somewhere. We got there and had a night of it. In the morning I couldn't remember how I'd got there, so that must qualify as a black-out and I thought, 'Wow, I need to start paying attention here.' It never got hold of me but I definitely noticed and heeded the warning.

I had some pretty wild times in the motorhome as well as some quiet, solitary times where I could reflect on who I really was – or at least who I was becoming; just gradually shedding all the negative connotations that society burdens being gay with. I guess I was lost.

Lost and flailing or lost and finding? The idea of finding oneself by getting lost has a lovely free-wheeling feel to it, does it not? Like Jack Kerouac riding the freight box cars across America but without the hardship. Time is all we've really got and much as this trip could sound like just like a rich man's indulgence, you can't help feeling that actually it was almost certainly the best therapy he could have given himself, reclaiming the carefree adolescence he never had, the part where he might normally have been expected to have found who he was and become comfortable with that. All those years squeezed into a jaunt as the true Andy finally began to take full-form right there in the motorhome beneath the solar panels.

At this point I guess I'd retired as far as having a career was concerned. I was still writing songs and recording them in my mini-studio, but creating songs is just what I do. It definitely wasn't for any planned album or project at this time and the idea of performing in front of people was by now completely off the agenda. It can be horribly painful to see yourself through the eyes of others if you're not comfortable with who you are. Anything you perceive as shortcomings are magnified and you either have to change them or accept them. Unless, of course, you choose to be oblivious to them through substance abuse and I'm sure that's one of the reasons there's such a high incidence of that in this business. People hate dishonesty even more than homosexuality and I have to be open and up-front; hence to have gone on stage before I'd resolved my issues would have been suicidal.

I really was as free as a bird. Besides, songwriting is very therapeutic – and in a way it has made music more sacred for me because it's not just a craft that you use for fame and fortune. It's so much more than that and when just used and abused in that way you sell out to yourself. I want some sort of sanctuary and I can find it in music.

I think that's one of the roles of music. I also think it's down to the artist to be as open and honest about one's own imperfections, fears, as he can be, express them, and encourage others to do likewise. It's universal once you get past the barrier of any particular language; everyone can relate to a beat and then it's just a spiritual communication. Music or any form of art just expresses a spirit, already out there and the artist channels it – through his own particular set of experiences and perceptions, filters. But the source, the spirit, is universal. I'm totally convinced of that.

People get that squashed out of them by all sorts of things – schools, work, society, whatever – and they succumb and forget. But it's still in there and the artist's role is to bring it out by being a sort of divining rod for the spirit that's there all around us throughout the universe. You get little reminders sometimes. Once I was sitting outside a beach cafe in Bali and something flew into my head, like a bird or something, and I couldn't work out what it was. Then it happened again, and again. Then I turned around and there was a kid of about four who had been ducking behind a small wall after he banged me on the head, full of glee, like God himself laughing that he'd tricked me. I exploded with laughter and we shared such a magical moment, a kid on the other side of the world communicating in such a universal way, like the universe having its own little giggle.

The motorhome adventure came to its natural conclusion. I'd ended up in Long Beach and was parked outside one of the bigger gay bars there. I'd bumped into this really good looking guy, we'd gone back to the motorhome and had a hell of a time, really good fun. I became infatuated with this guy for quite some time afterwards. But he had no conception of a relationship; there was never any response mentally from him, just a few more sexual encounters. Anyway, it caused me to hang around Long Beach for quite a long time and I decided to buy a condo there by the beach – and that's when I sold the motorhome. Gave away the motorbike I had on the back of it too, hoped the kid didn't kill himself on it.

It was during this time that I first encountered a major influence on my life subsequently, an older gay man called David. He looked like Santa Claus, big white beard – and was very wise. He came from a farming community in Ohio where to be gay was totally unthinkable, so he'd relocated to Long Beach, originally with his boyfriend to start a life together but it hadn't worked out. He made his living buying and selling rental properties but seemed to organise his life around doing people favours. It seemed like it was his mission to help young gays with the process of coming out. He was very instrumental in my life and psychological state in guiding me through in a very slow and subtle way. Instead of telling me things, he'd nudge me along by just asking me questions – I guess based on his own experience of coming out years earlier. We'd take a lot of lunches and dinners together and just sit and talk. He'd casually say, 'There's a good looking guy,' and we'd sit and discuss things. He'd ask, say, how I felt about such and such type of sex, what did I think about that guy over there and it wasn't so much the questions themselves, or him needing to know, but a feeling that for the first time I could openly express such things, feel comfortable about them and crack a joke or whatever, and hear myself saying such things, and the sky not fall in. There was no judgmental army to jump in with long-held stigmas. Over a period of time, such thoughts and ways became more normalised, and self-acceptance began. When I first met David there was still no way I could ever conceive of being publicly gay but gradually that became more and more feasible thanks to his help.

I then met a guy at Long Beach who was to become my partner for the next seven years. It was at the beach, he had a plaster cast on his leg, had broken it skiing, and that gave a conversation-opener. The relationship built and became more serious and I began to feel more and more confident and positive about coming out. He wasn't at that stage yet but he was a decent guy, very loyal and honest. I was already beginning to feel a bit hemmed-in at the apartment. I was always very conscious of how much noise I could make in my studio there because of the neighbours and I wanted to be able to make a lot of noise. So we began to look at getting a place together.

Just when things were looking up, when a path seemed finally to be opening, the struggle being won, came fate uninvited. A cough, a hacking cough...

ALL RIGHT NOW

The encounter that did the damage was almost certainly during the hedonistic motorhome odyssey. It's not a subject Andy will dwell on and it's easy to understand why: it happened and you can't turn back the clock.

You step across a line. You realise there is no going back to the other side of that line. I don't know which liaison gave me the infection and in a way it doesn't matter. Somewhere along the line I had failed to take responsibility in the heat of the moment and this was the result of that lack of vigilance. There was no excuse; this was the early 1990s, AIDS was already very well publicised and you could not fail to be aware of the risks. There's no way of telling how long I had the HIV virus before I began to get symptoms, so the possibilities of the source were virtually endless.

I felt very sick. It felt like the worst 'flu I'd ever had, hacking and coughing, a fever that sucks all the life out you. I went to the doc and it turned out to be hepatitis B. But they wanted to test me for a whole bunch of other things including HIV and it came back positive. You become frozen. It's almost like a kick in the gut, and you realise you've taken a step and there's no going back. No matter how much you desperately want to cross back to the other side of that line, you can't. I hate to be prideful, but I observed how quickly I thought, 'OK, we have much less time than we thought.' You quickly realise what's important and what's not and cut out all the shit. I removed myself emotionally from the effects of it...

'I removed myself emotionally from the effects of it' is a characteristically Andy downplaying of a monumental task. The enormity of doing just that – to not let emotions cloud the realisation that you might be about to prematurely lose your life – is given short thrift because it will simply get in the way of what needs to be done. So cut it out. Imagine the self-control needed to do that. In the tough, streetwise little hustler in control of his destiny from an early age and answering to no-one, who then spurned the almost limitless opportunities to over-indulge in order to keep the big picture in its correct context can be seen already the remarkable qualities that he would now need to call upon for an altogether tougher task.

... but there are several devastating physical things in between, and it was the physical pain that really got to me. Every day I'd scrape myself out of bed, force myself to have a shower and struggle to find a new reason not to kill myself. Yet even though suicide was definitely in my thoughts from time to time, I actually never felt as desperate as during the time when I'd previously considered it – when I was struggling to come to terms with being gay. That had actually left me in a worse state mentally than this – which might give you some idea of how desperate the gay struggle was. This time it was only the physical pain and suffering and actually mentally I was in a stronger place.

It was like this for about three years – until they started making some headway with the medication. It was complicated by the fact that at the same time I had crippling pain in my neck and arms – to the point where playing the bass seemed already to be in the past tense. It later turned out this was an issue related to the drugs treatment but it took a long time for this diagnosis to be arrived at. In the meantime I had painful disc surgery that was completely ineffective – and after which they were saying they could see nothing physically wrong with my back or neck. You can't imagine what it's like having someone telling you that when you are in agony from it. There was clearly something very wrong; aside from the pain, I'd go into the gym and be sweating like crazy yet my feet felt like blocks of ice. Living with that level of physical pain day after day really does eat into your energy and resolve.

The HIV virus causes damage to the immune system and opportunistic infections strike, and when an HIV patient has any two from a long list of symptoms they are said to have AIDS. The hepatitis B was the first outward sign for Andy. Subsequently he would develop Kaposi's Sarcoma – black cancerous growths on the skin that confirmed he now had full-blown AIDS. He suffered thirty-five episodes of these, painstakingly having each removed before the cancer could develop into anything immediately life-threatening. Most of them were on his torso but he jokes that he really took it personally when he got one on his face: 'Shows that vanity remains even in the toughest of times!' Most have left no visible trace and he's had a couple of tattoos engraved over the ones on his arm that did leave a scar and a few on his back.

Meantime the doctors did what they could with what was available at the time. The drugs industry has made massive progress in AIDS-related medication in the two decades since then but in the early stages of Andy's illness it was still very crude.

Initially it was something called AZT which was pretty much all they had, an awful drug. Then they added a few more, one that is known to cause a lot of residual nerve damage and that triggered the peripheral neuropathy that turned out to be what was behind my terrible neck pain. The drugs back then were devastating in themselves. Some, when you first start taking them, gave a skin rash so severe that death is actually possible in the first two weeks. The rash is everywhere, including the eyelids. If you survived the first two weeks of the drug you were good to continue but that wasn't by any means assured and in the meantime you were a head-to-toe pus-ball.

Sometime later my doctor at the time favoured cutting back on the meds and following a more homeopathic route, which we did for quite some time. Each visit it would be 'OK, we fixed that; now you've got this wrong with you,' and mentally I was fine with that and would just say, 'OK, what do we do about that?' Spiritually I was in great shape. Because of the spiritual belief I had come to, I was not in any way afraid of death, nor the pain of death, though maybe a prolonged painful death wouldn't have been so welcome. Sometimes in fact I would have welcomed the relief from the physical pain that a quick death would have brought. In a way it was sort of a preparation for what comes next, after this life.

Discussing, say, the attitude of homophobes or recent foreign policy of the USA or the blinkered attitudes within the music industry, Andy may say something along the lines of, 'Sometimes I think I'll be glad to get to the next planet. Fucking idiots on this one!' But said with a twinkling smile, and an amused 'mmm', the same smile and sound, the same calm in the eyes you can see in the eighteen-year-old Andy when being interviewed on Australian TV and he's talking about the destruction that sometimes befell Free's amps on stage – when life must have seemed a whole lot simpler but maybe paradoxically more mystifying. Those calm eyes have stared into the brink since then, so often you sense it's become a territory that's actually familiar. You quite believe him when he says it holds no fears for him.

There was a period where it didn't look like I was coming back. I was getting progressively more ill. This was when my antibody count was down to one T-cell and my viral load was 3.4 million. When your viral load gets over 10,000 they want you on medication so these were just insane numbers, numbers that the doctors hadn't even seen before, and it was seemingly going only in one direction. Although the doctors never said so, they didn't need to. I could sense them silently climbing the walls and thinking, 'What the hell do we try next?' I looked severely ill, skeletal, and no matter how positive I tried to be, when you go out for a walk and all you can do afterwards is go back to bed to recover, you get the idea that there may not be much time left. But part of my brain was still hanging on.

From the initial diagnosis to this stage covered a period of about three years; regular blood transfusions, in and out of hospital, physical agony in between. The main thing I recall about my hospital visits were the throat cancer victims going outside for a smoke, inhaling through a hole in their throat! That's addiction for you.

My doctor of the time went ever-deeper into my specific symptoms and sought out deeper advice until eventually we found the right specialist. From there we began making progress; slow at first, as we found what worked, what didn't, what needed to be fine-tuned. At the same time there was a lot of progress with retroviral drugs. But the big breakthrough for me personally was correctly diagnosing the peripheral neuropathy and the drugs causes behind it. This was occurring around the disc area and radiating out from there, which is why they originally thought the discs were the problem. The 'frozen feet' were a symptom of the numbing of the nerves, something many diabetics end up with. The feet were helped immensely by monthly IVIG and the neck nerves are now controlled by Valium. I never got a kick from Valium the way some people do but it just keeps me relaxed enough that the nerves don't get irritated and the muscles don't go into spasm.

Just getting that under control was a monumental step for me because although I was still weak and sick, the pain was hugely reduced. From there I was like a new person and I could begin to think about exercising. I was fortunate enough in my circumstances that as I got fitter I had the time to do up to six hours of exercise each day. As my fitness levels came up, I was able to get that down to about three hours a day. That was, and remains, very necessary not just for my general health but also to keep my body from seizing up as a side-effect of the drugs. There was one particular drug I had for a time which was great, the closest thing to acid you could imagine with a really nice buzz. But like most drugs you end up chewing your lip waiting for the next hit and it was getting out of control, I was getting like a speed freak – so I had to come off it, which was a shame.

For the last eight years I've been pretty much good to go. They finessed the treatment and I'm incredibly closely monitored. From 3.4 million, my viral load is now undetectable, but one shouldn't think of that as 'gone'. I'm an incredibly lucky guy. Lucky that the drugs and treatment improved in time, lucky we found the right guy, lucky I could afford to pay for the treatment, lucky I could afford the time for the exercise. My insurance covers much of the cost but in addition I spend about 30 grand a year on treatment, which is a fair exchange as far as I'm concerned. I have something called intravenous haemoglobin, a very refined blood product, every two weeks for an hour. Stick a needle in the arm, lie back and watch a movie. That's $5,000 a time, so you can see how it adds up.

You have to give a lot of credit to those ACT UP guys that campaigned for improved treatment in the early days, that were really in your face in a very aggressive way, bringing attention to the issue, fighting a cause on your behalf and really forcing the situation. I'm sure if that sort of pressure was put on cancer medication there would be a huge improvement.

See Andy today and it seems scarcely believable that he was ever so ill. He's a poster boy for health and fitness, looks like a guy in his late-forties who fitness trains incessantly and lives in the sunshine of California – great colour, not an ounce of flab, well-defined and toned, his movements quick and lithe. Truly miraculous and actually inspiring when you spend any time dwelling on what he's been through. It's left no visible scar either on his body or psyche. In fact, he even believes it's strengthened him.

It's made for a very healthy stripping-away process. When you have to let everything go, even to the extent that you've given up on staying alive, you really get to understand the essence of everything and what is important. There's a positive aspect to everything, nothing is intrinsically good or bad. Cars are good in that they get you from A to B but aren't so good if B is a tree! So do you ban cars? Do you ban drugs? Drugs have brought enlightenment but also create addiction and dependency. Nothing is only good or only bad, it's all about how it is used. Even the pain that Free's break-up caused me was because they had set a standard in my life and I left because we were no longer maintaining that standard as a band.

I've never shied away from challenge. Why the hell leave Free, a band with the best singer in the world, when you can hardly sing? Just why would you do that? So I know about challenges and the illness was a big one, no question. I have a fuller appreciation of life having been so close to death. I have always been focussed, ever since my early teens, but it was only after this that I became truly focussed. That was as nothing compared to now. All my questions have been answered, I know for sure my purpose, know what to dismiss, what to take seriously. Anything that was vague before no longer is. I know what I'm supposed to do, why and sort of how. I'm on that road. I can get outside myself and see a bigger picture. I'm fifty-seven now and I don't feel it at all, feel like I'm in my thirties. Considering everything I've been through I should feel like eighty-seven. I might not have as long to live as I would have if I'd not had the illness but I'm pretty confident I'll out-live most of my contemporaries.

One thing very noticeable about Andy is that he is not up for wasting time. It's a finite resource – for all of us, not just Andy. But he's acutely aware of it, having stared death in the face, won't countenance non-productive use of the gift that is time. Even the idea of having to sleep a third of his life away irritates him. Decisions are made quickly, tasks identified and pursued. He's full-on from the moment he gets up at 5 in the morning to begin his exercise regime until 8.30 in the evening when he retires. A visit to the bathroom is an opportunity to catch up on e-mail, a phone-caller has about five seconds in which to identify themselves before they're cut short. He watches the TV news and current affairs programmes as he's doing his sit-ups in the mornings and will have it on in the background as he's preparing his high-protein lunch.

Is it a lonely existence in his rock star pad? Well, his daughters are constantly in touch, and he works closely with them even though until recently they were in Australia. Both are now in California, Hannah in Hollywood pursuing a modelling career and her environmental 'mermaid' campaign and Jasmine with her peers in Silicon Valley where her computer-programming talents are at home. On a day-to-day level he's friendly with a lot of the locals – the staff of the restaurants all greet him enthusiastically, like a returning friend. He's on good, chatty terms with the neighbourhood's gardeners and pool cleaners. But there's no longer a partner to share his life.

No, he lived here for seven years. We were together when I bought this place, moved up from Long Beach together. But he wasn't helping me move on. He had this straight life at work and then this fantasy gay life in complete seclusion here with me that his straight colleagues knew nothing about – and he wasn't ready to come out, was very closeted. He liked to tend to the gardens, the trees and bushes, driving the mini-tractor around, pretending to be a farmer. It was great for him but wasn't helping me. He was a decent guy, had a lot of positive aspects but I was starting to write coming out songs and planning what eventually became the *Naked And Finally Free* album; it was time to get real and he wasn't prepared to be on that journey. He was actually hindering my coming out process.

I recall one night we went to a comedy club in Palm Springs together and the comedian said, 'Any gays in here?' not expecting anyone to put their hands up. But I did, said, 'Yeah, I'm gay,' smiling, thinking, 'Go on, you fucker. Do your gay joke now.' And he didn't, just moved right on. But I think my partner was pretty uncomfortable with that. Thinking about it, he liked country and western music – that should have been a deal-breaker right from the start!

Cue the 'mmm' and the smiling, happy brown eyes. In answer to that earlier question: no; he doesn't give off any vibe of loneliness.

I find I'm actually happier alone than when I was in the relationship. I live in splendid isolation, though I'm in touch with everyone important to me thanks to the wonders of modern electronic communication. I'm not big on gay bars as I don't really feel part of that 'You go, girl' stuff and I'm not actively looking for a partner. I have no particular need for there to be anyone else – ironically even for sex, something I fought so hard for. It's impossible to tell a young person that, because God has made sure we've got a sex drive – survival of the species. It's hard for them to understand that even though you can still enjoy it when you're older, you have the ability not to be ruled by your dick. I'm not lonely in the least here, I can be perfectly content in my own space. That said, I'm not closed to the idea of a partner. I think it would probably have to be someone in the same business though, someone that could be integrated into what I'm doing, who supported the cause. I don't want to have to stop my life to take them to the movies or whatever.

'Serenely busy' is about the best way of describing Andy's situation. Very little interrupts that equilibrium. But there is one thing that can still get beneath his skin: the subject of Paul Rodgers. It's something that needs revisiting when discussing this stage of his life, for in 1994 after the pain from the peripheral neuropathy had been fixed, but whilst still heavily into his recovery programme, Andy got a call out of the blue from Rodgers, asking if he might be available to play with him at Woodstock. This wasn't a Free reunion – Simon Kirke wasn't on drums and there were other non-Free-related guests – but it nonetheless would be the first time the two creative driving forces of that band had performed together since the split. From the outside, for the Free fans, it was an intriguing, enticing prospect. Even Andy, determinedly in the present Andy, was intrigued.

He phoned and, unusually for him, got straight to the point: would I be up for doing it? I agreed immediately, even though the timing was actually very awkward for me because it was in the middle of a five-day process at a hospital in Lake Tahoe where they take your blood, re-oxygenate it and recycle it back in an attempt to clean it of the infections. It was quite a serious piece of treatment and to just take a weekend out of that to go to New York to play Woodstock wasn't ideal, or particularly easy for me at that time. But Paul had played a big part in giving me the strength and integrity that formed me and though somewhere along the line he had seemingly abandoned those artistic values and made a different choice, I said yes to Woodstock for no other reason than I wanted to see where he was at now.

It wasn't a happy experience. The first hint that it might be difficult came when I received a cassette tape in the post from him and a note saying I should learn the songs on there. Fucker – I wrote half of them! There were some Bad Company numbers too and he'd also invited Slash to do a couple of numbers and Brian May. Jason Bonham was on drums, I was on bass. I've a feeling I was second choice, actually, like someone had let him down at the last moment. It wasn't in any way a Free thing, other than we did 'All Right Now' and a couple of others. It was just Paul Rodgers with a band and we were all treated accordingly.

We stayed in Manhattan and had two days of rehearsal. Brian May was there on the first day but he left when it became clear that we weren't going to be doing any Queen numbers. Brian was immensely pissed off by that and rang my room saying how bad he thought it was – and that he was on the next plane home. I was back in very familiar and unwelcome territory from the latter days of Free: when Paul decides what he's doing and has an agenda, he never explicitly says it. He would just have allowed Brian to think one thing by not contradicting him until he'd got him there: plausible deniability. I just accepted it because it was nothing to do with me, but I could see exactly what was happening.

Paul and I have never actually had our grievances out. Our relationship has always been most civil, perhaps too civil. Maybe if we had had it out it would have been good for everybody. Free was such a vibe band you'd just pick up what everyone else was thinking. It's maybe a weakness of mine that instead of having it out I just moved on and it's maybe a weakness that I've never talked it through with him.

He didn't know what I was going through in terms of my treatment but we were so distant that to have talked about that wasn't conceivable. Even at rehearsals there was no sense of being close. As for the gig itself, I was there only as 'the bass player' – just like the last days of Free. Seemed to me Paul was in exactly the same place after all that time. So at least I had my answer on that score.

On the day of the performance Paul presented everyone with a two-page contract numbered P. 43 and 44. I said these need to be re-numbered 1 and 2, or we need to see and sign off on pages 1-42. A big kerfuffle ensued, with Paul's girlfriend arguing on the phone with my attorney in California about law. If ever there was a *Spinal Tap* moment, this was it. Sitting back and watching this I was in disbelief how we could ever have ended up like this. Just the kinda vibe we needed to take on stage...

In the history of rock music missed opportunities, that Woodstock '94 gig has got to be right up near the top. Here were the two primary driving forces of one of the greatest bands of all time re-united after a split of twenty-two years – and it was completely diluted by bringing in others unconnected with the band, and by placing Andy in the role of almost unseen session musician. It evidently wasn't in Paul Rodgers' mind that this was any sort of Free re-union, but how could it not be once he'd invited Andy? Or was it a deliberate snubbing of Free's significance, a sort of implicit assumption that Paul Rodgers was bigger than Free? And that therefore his act of placing Andy in the role of support musician all those years ago was justified?

From the outside, it's the most bizarre relationship, still frozen in a conflict of forty years ago that has never been articulated by either party to the other. Yet, however unspoken and old that conflict is, it remains absolutely radioactive even though they are, nominally at least, still on quite civilised speaking terms. Simon Kirke – who still plays with Rodgers whenever Bad Company reconvenes to tour – keeps well out the way, refuses publicly to take sides. In the making of this book Andy was completely cool with – even encouraging of – me contacting Paul to give his side of things. Several unanswered e-mails later it was clear Rodgers had no intention of talking on this subject.

It started, who knows where, sometime in 2002 and it spread like wildfire over the internet: Andy Fraser, bass player and songwriter with the legendary '70s band Free had died from AIDS. 'Yeah, I got a call from a music journalist saying, "Dude, I'm just about to write your obituary. So it's not true, then?"' Andy hadn't at that stage gone public with his condition or his sexuality. Ironically, by the time the rumour emerged, he was well on the way to physical recovery. So if he was setting the record straight on one, it seemed only right he should do it on the other too. From this sprungNaked And Finally Free, Andy's 'coming out' album, released in 2005.

Yeah, I had to respond first of all to that story, let everyone know that the reports of my demise were greatly exaggerated! The journalist that phoned me had been talking to another musician and mentioned my 'death' and the musician said, 'No way that's true. I was talking to him yesterday.' Prior to that whole thing, in my mind I'd basically retired. I was still writing stuff but it was for my own expression, not for putting out there. But this jolted me into it. It's one thing saying, 'Hey, no, I'm still here,' but really I felt the need to say more than that. I wanted to show just *how* alive, not only, 'I'm still here,' but, 'I'm still here and this is who I am now.' I don't actually know how the death rumour started. I'd guess that someone knew I had AIDS, someone else said my career was dead and things got mixed up. You'd drive yourself crazy trying to track everything down written about you that was incorrect. Even now, my birthday is listed wrongly everywhere. For the record, it's July 3, 1952, not August 7.

That internet rumour dragged a public persona of Andy frozen in the early 1970s bang into the present. From afar, it could almost be a different person. Close up, spending time with him, the progression from teenage rock star to gay man in his fifties makes perfect sense. But the outside world has only his published output to go on and on that level there is a huge disconnect between Free or even the early Andy Fraser Band and Naked And Finally Free. *Had his solo career developed in the '80s the way, say, Steve Winwood's had, or had 'Every Kinda People' lit up his own career rather than Robert Palmer's, then that progression would be more obvious. But the picture presented in* Naked And Finally Free *was, from the outside, startling. Not only was the music apparently unconnected with what the average Free fan would recognise, but here was the man saying he was gay too!*

Not only fans but even people you know get familiar with one picture of you – and then you change that picture completely when you come out. Musically, it was very important that I be myself. It wasn't worth doing if I wasn't going to be completely honest – and of course the natural follow-on from that was coming out on record. After everything I'd been through I felt much more comfortable about being myself in my music.

Coming out is obviously a big thing for anyone, but for me now that I was comfortable with myself, I wanted to end the fear of being outed, to live life as an open book and be free of secrets. Also, I felt a responsibility to help do away with the stigma, by giving a broader face to being gay than the obvious stereotypical image. The album was a very effective way of doing this.

The songs are highly personal, with explicit candour in place of the generic lyrics of his earlier work. The bouncy, joy-filled reggae groove within him is expressed freely throughout but can contrast with the hard-hitting messages in many of the songs – in exactly the same way the easy sheen of Andy's personality can disguise some pretty cutting observations.

That style of lyric-writing has just evolved with my own growth. In my initial songwriting I was very influenced by Paul Rodgers. He loves double entendres but also had a skilful simplicity with words, like 'Be my friend, I will love you to the very end'. That's very direct. In my writing now I want to have that directness but without being clever-cutesy or vague. I want to lay it on the line and although there's a risk it becomes too in your face, there's a risk with everything.

'Healing Hands' kicks the album off and lends the CD its distinctive cover image, a hand rising from the water, seemingly a last call for help. It was designed by Andy's elder daughter Hannah, a very gifted artist. The four long fingers might also be taken as the strings of the bass, though Andy says that hadn't occurred to him.

'Healing Hands' was my calling out to God, I guess. Not only because of my physical pain at the time but also to let Him know I was calling out, just a prayer really. Throughout this album I'm dealing with two of rock 'n' roll's three 'no-go' zones – God and gayness. All I have to do is write about guns too and I'll have all three!

'Yours Faithfully' deals explicitly with Andy's struggle with and acceptance of AIDS. It's written in the form of a letter to a lover.

That's kind of a coming out message, a public letter written in the form of a private one. The message is that desire can still overwhelm me, that there's a mountain I need to climb but I'm going for it. That song germinated over a long time. The reggae groove underneath finally revealed itself and for a long time I was fiddling around with the lyrics. I had the melody first and was just singing what I heard in terms of vowel sounds, but I hadn't quite locked into a theme and initially the lyrics didn't mean anything. Then suddenly it struck me where I was going with it, so I was able to twist them around a little until they made sense. It's sometimes like that, as if you are half-intuiting the universe but either through your own limitations or blockages you haven't let your guard down enough to be as open as you need to be – so you're only getting fragments. Although they don't seem to mean anything when you look at those fragments, they do have a value. It's like a jigsaw puzzle until you suddenly lock onto the universal picture. It's a process that always amuses me. Other songs come complete. You just wake up and they're already there.

'Stand Ready' is not so much a call to arms to the gay community as Andy's confirmation that he is with them. Like the other songs on the record, it succeeds in being true to who he is without resorting to caricature gay.

It's me saying, 'I'm with you, ready to do the right thing. If there's a fight, I'm there, standing alongside you. I'm ready after all those years of not acknowledging it, that all the bullshit is stripped away and I've got real and have committed.' I guess I've continued that theme on 'Too Far To Turn Back Now', which was a song that was a long time germinating. The title sums up how I feel about my life – that I've started out down this road and I'm going to just keep going, that I'm committed even if I make an idiot of myself. I'm talking to the gay community I suppose but not directly. The gay issue happens to have made itself my issue and has been a sort of focus by which I measure things, but the things that make you human, the differences and imperfections, could be about anything. It's more about embracing who we are than the specific gay thing. The things that make each of us unique are the things that make us useful and valuable and as teenagers – and even afterwards for many people – we try to fit in with the gang but if we can be bold enough to open up to our imperfections, we grow. The sentiments could be transferred to any other issue and that's consistent with my wish that the world gets past the gay / straight thing and why I'm not into making a big flamboyant statement about it. I understand the Gay Pride marches but that's not where I feel my best role would be served. If the guy with the beard and pink trousers wants to wave his placard from the back of the truck to get on the news, fine. But I feel I could be of more use doing what I'm doing here. Everyone does what they can and my contribution is addressing the issue in my work.

'Don't Leave' is a wistful song, longing for someone for company. I rarely feel lonely but I did on this particular day. It was germinated in the motorhome days when I was yearning for a partner at the time. I can see now I sort of chickened out lyrically with that one. Where I say, 'I do believe I'm falling in love for the first time in my life,' – which I wasn't, actually – I was originally going to say, 'I want to be wrapped in love's all-consuming fire,' which is out of the Bible, I think.

'Jungle' casts Andy in the role of social commentator on the world around him and is unrelated in its content to the coming out theme, as though he's already moving on from that even within the coming out record.

I read the words somewhere 'It's a jungle out there,' and they just suggested themselves immediately as a song title. Even just those words suggest their own rhythm and melody, so it quickly fell into a groove and I ended up sort of riffing about the news items of that time – kids in gangs, gun shots in the night, Matthew Shepherd's torture, skinheads in Texas dragging a black guy behind a pick-up truck to his death, a doctor who'd performed abortions being shot and killed by a 'pro-lifer' as he was sitting at his home, conspiracy plots, chat rooms. It's a jungle out there – a concrete jungle but a jungle all the same. I was just trying to be a newscaster though I never felt I quite nailed the role. The best I've seen anyone pull that off was Marvin Gaye in 'What's Going On'.

'Hands Of Time' is a song of regret for the hurt I caused Ri, saying sorry I made her cry but that I can't turn back the hands of time and can only go forwards. I'll be paying for my mistakes to my grave and there's definitely an element of personal therapy about this song and a few of the others. It's a way of getting things off my chest and that's part of the artist's job. When you express your imperfections and regrets it provokes a human reaction and the listener can maybe relate that to things in their own lives and that's got to be healthy. As a performer if you don't provoke a human reaction you're failing in your job.

'Deliverance' is the most overtly spiritual thing I've put down on record, an expression of how I'm no longer afraid of death, that at times I'm actually welcoming it, waiting to be delivered, burdens falling away like burst bubbles. Again, this is tricky subject matter in the mind of the music business but I think people are a lot more astute than the industry gives them credit for. People are more than capable of enjoying stuff that's not just fairy tale pap, running through fields of gold etc. That's the default position of the music industry, the safe place it always retreats to and it takes an artist who's already successful doing that stuff to stand up and say, 'OK, now we're going to do something a little more edgy and dangerous,' like The Beatles did – and it was still vastly successful. Yet the business never has embraced that lesson.

I like the sentiment of the title of 'Someone Watching Over Me', because that's how it's always felt. I've always just trusted things to take care of themselves and they always have. You get some challenges along the way, of course. 'Family' is all about my girls and how I feel about them, how we still keep the fire alive. When they lived in Australia we'd go on trips and we'd often end up at these hippy-type beach parties with bonfires and guitars where that idea of keeping the flame alive seemed very appropriate. They will always have sanctuary here, whatever shit they may encounter.

'The Night' is a straightforward lust song, though I tried to do it in a poetic way. It's ended up a sort of reggae/jazz amalgam in style and I could actually hear Paul singing it. 'Standing At Your Window' is the odd one out on the album in that I wrote it many years ago for Frankie Miller. I did about ten songs for him and he recorded maybe six. This was one of the ones he left out and this version is also on the Frankie benefit album where lots of different artists sing his songs. Frankie originally wrote the lyrics but in this version I've changed the verses. The idea of him standing by your window calling to you is just so Frankie, much more him than me.

As I listen to this record in more detail, in the context of Andy's struggle, and with his talking me through it, there's something incredibly moving about the spirit of dignified defiance, something in keeping with the best aspects of the human condition. But you'd need to understand all he's been through and the courage of his calls to properly appreciate the emotional intensity at the core of the work, coated as it is in his sunny presentation. It is, of course, a piece of work deep in significance in Andy's life in that it finally reveals to the world who he really is. Implicit in that is the explanation of his long absence from public view and he is saying, 'Here is who I am now. You may like it, you may not but I can't be anything else. Take it or leave it.'

Having made the big decision to put that message out there, reaction to the gay issue was actually fairly muted. The record got good reviews but there was no big sensation created by the message. I got many letters from gay fans thanking me for standing up and being counted – which was half the reason for coming out – but there was no other particular reaction. If anyone thought anything negative they didn't dare say it. Sometime later when I did the song supporting Obama, people were much more openly hostile. I would guess those guys would also be homophobic but maybe they find themselves having to bite their tongues these days on the gay issue. People use the M-word (Muslim) on Obama, I guess because they don't feel they can use the N-word – but they mean the same thing by it. So I'm aware there's probably a whole swathe of people like that who would actually be very hostile to the coming out message in the record, but who haven't made their point public.

In terms of my friends, no-one said anything. Does it mean that some may just quietly cease contact because of it? Possibly, and that's one of the things you have to consider when coming out.

I'd already had the conversation with the girls, well before I came out publicly. They'd called me separately, with a little gap in between, and it was clear that they'd spoken to each other. I recognised they were asking me stuff through adult eyes, like I had tried with my father, getting no satisfactory answers, so I was completely open with them and we connected in a real way. Their reaction was definitely, 'Oh, is that all? We thought you'd split from mum because you didn't like her.' We had a good laugh about that, it felt like they wrapped their arms around me from the other side of the world and they really didn't see it as a big deal. Ri had never disclosed the details of our split with the girls and she's to be credited for that, and for being a great mother to them. She was always very good about maintaining a positive father image of me. Even if the father doesn't deserve that, it's a good thing to do because the kid deserves it and there was never any negativity towards me from the girls.

As for Paul and Simon, we've never spoken about my coming out although with Simon it's been acknowledged. When we were together for the *Free Forever* release in London it was obviously out in the open but it didn't seem to be anything we needed to expand upon. I don't know whether or not Paul would think negatively about it but if he did it would kind of amuse me, given that he fronts Queen in place of Freddy Mercury and, if for no other reason than that, would have to be very careful with what he said!

With the release of the 2006 Free Forever *DVD celebrating the band, came a notion of a one-off Free reunion. But that old radioactivity came right back to nix the idea – maybe for the best. Andy's still not sure of the full story, knows only that Rodgers' manager phoned and mentioned the idea to him, asked him what he thought of a one-off gig.*

In the past I'd been very negative to the idea of it, but on this occasion I took a deep breath and said if we were ever going to do it, this would be the time. There were outside suggestions for it too and I did speak to both Paul and Simon about the idea of a filmed gig we could put on the DVD and really do a proper job of it. Basically Simon was up for it and Paul wasn't. But his manager kept calling and saying, 'Call Paul, he's expecting your call, set up a time,' and it was like a done thing, so I rang and Paul just said, 'What? I don't know what you're talking about.' It felt kinda ugly. Back in the day we got on so well because we each had something that the others needed at the time. I don't think that's the case anymore. I don't think Paul wants anyone around that would do anything other than what he says and it's much better for him to pay a sideman who plays the right notes and never opens his mouth. Which isn't me.

I don't hold it against him that he didn't want to do a gig together – I didn't really either, to be honest. But what I don't get is all the subterfuge around it that created an awkward situation unnecessarily. I'm sure there's a part of Paul that says, 'I don't need to,' and yes, fine. But it was as if he wanted to prove that point. It was a similar story with the release of the DVD in London, for which the three of us were supposed to show up. Simon and I made it, Paul didn't. He was going to be coming, then he wasn't and in the end his son and daughter represented him and he did a phone hook-up for a few minutes, giving some very unconvincing answers to the fans' questions. It left a bad aftertaste and many people giggling.

See footage of that get-together and it looks like Andy, Simon and the fans are all digging a rather magical situation, each riffing off the other, the fans genuinely fascinated to hear their stories, approaching afterwards on a human level for an autograph or two, a long way removed from the teenagers trying to rip their clothes from their bodies and their hair from their heads back in the day. But it's true it would have been so much more moving and powerful had the other surviving member been there too. 'A couple of times as Paul gave some or other answer on his phone link Simon and I would exchange glances and raise our eyebrows, in a gesture of "Really? That's not how I recall it." Mmm.' Yeah, Andy's half-bemused, half-amused by the whole situation, but there it is again, that itch in Andy's being that is Paul Rodgers, the young dude the Free front man was, the public approval-junkie he apparently became and how that changed the course of Free, from what it could have been to the brilliant but brief thing it was, the major impact that that had on Andy's trajectory. It's as if everything else in Andy's life – his sexuality, his relationship with his daughters, his divorce, his rebirth as a published recording artist, his coming out – has been resolved, but there remains one thing that has not: Andy, Paul and their awkward, civilised, seething, unresolved forty-year issues. Lennon and McCartney split and had a sometimes-vicious public spat that lasted maybe eighteen months in the immediate aftermath of the end of The Beatles, but with that out the way there was a rapprochement. Jagger and Richards have some four-decades-old mutual jealousy about various women that has permanently bruised their relationship but they still rub along somehow. Page and Plant have a continuing competitive resentment, thirty years on from the end of Zeppelin, but have made music together since and still don't rule out collaborating again. Yet four decades on, the two creative forces of Free – the band that was dubbed 'The New Stones' but which now somehow seems from a time way before the Stones – still haven't even mutually acknowledged they have stuff to discuss.

From the outside, having spent time with Andy, got to fit right in with the easy cadences of his personality, seen his unassuming being out in the world like a regular real guy, it's hard not to side with him, even without having the benefit of Paul Rodgers' take. See, as a devastated, thirteen-year-old Free fan I didn't much recognise the Paul Rodgers of Free in Bad Company '74 onwards. Yes, I recognised the wonderful voice, could hear the obvious catchy, driving commercial power of 'Can't Get Enough' (a Mick Ralphs song) but where was the magical mix of power and soul of Free? I couldn't hear it. I can see and hear the Paul Rodgers of Bad Company in Queen, separated by thirty-six years. But between Free and Bad Company, separated by just a few months, I couldn't, and can't, get the link. It was like a great artist had cashed in his chips – way, way too early. I feel a great affinity with Andy in so many things, I absolutely get him and his powerfully independent spirit and have huge admiration and respect for how he's conquered his obstacles. Put those things together and I'm naturally inclined towards Andy's take on things Free – and perhaps that's unfair on Paul Rodgers. There were no rules saying he had to continue to please the same set of fans that had been enraptured by Free, nothing saying his musical vision should fit with Andy's, nothing saying he shouldn't strive to maximise his commercial potential at the earliest opportunity and with the minimum of fuss. But the soul of the man who wrote and co-wrote with Andy such majestic, powerful, yet subtle material as on the Free albums is surely still in there – and Andy's surely owed a frank, cards-on-the-table, one-on-one, let's re-connect talk with that part of him, something that would take as long as it takes. That's the least he's owed. But maybe I'm biased. In the meantime, Rodgers is the trigger for some classically-Andy understated one-liners. When I tell him Paul has just done an interview with Classic Rock *magazine in which he manages to talk of Free without once mentioning Andy, he replies, 'Wish I could be so disciplined. Mmm.'*

In putting out Naked And Finally Free, *Andy didn't have to worry about getting a record deal this time around, such is the way the industry has developed. He simply put it out himself. He is the artist, producer and distributor all in one. Some of the accompanying musicians he has never even met. They send each other sound files by e-mail and Andy takes it from there, emphasising how it's such a different game today.*

In some ways being with a label would make it a lot easier for me. But that would be a bit of a weird trip because they're all losing money and looking for the next *American Idol* guy. I don't think an old gay guy is their idea of the easy way of doing it! For a while I had to have my head into organising getting albums duplicated, shipped in bulk to go to the next distribution outlet, overseeing t-shirts and stuff. That's a lot of shit to be dealing with when you're writing and playing full time. With Mctrax it is a lot more automated now. I'm not opposed to performing live but there's no way I could do it sitting in a car for eight hours a day, like we used to. A tour would need to be done properly and that's an expensive undertaking. I'm fifty-seven years old; you're no longer going to get me at Leeds one day, Amsterdam the next. You're not going to put me back in a van! I've done enough of that.

ALL RIGHT NOW

Writing about my big issue – my coming out – in *Naked And Finally Free* uncorked further material, even as I moved on from the actual coming out. Other things that are important to me have fuelled the fire lit by the making of that work.

'Take Me Home For Christmas' was a song about the issue of gays in the military. Funnily enough, I hate Christmas songs, or ninety per cent of them. It's when the Christmas whores come out and try to get some of those festive dollars. Many of the great singers I thought were singing from the heart in fact have proven it's all merely a skill and they could be singing about an 'oil and lube job' for the car. 'Take Me Home For Christmas' I dreamt, and on coming into consciousness with it ringing around my head I could only laugh and think, 'Somebody's got a sense of humour,' and just had to go with it.

There is a policy backed by federal law of 'don't ask/don't tell' (DADT) which restricts the military's attempts at uncovering closet gays and lesbians but which bars those who are openly gay. The policy's wording prohibits those who 'demonstrate a propensity or intent to engage in homosexual acts' from serving because it 'would create an unacceptable risk to the high standards of morale, good order and discipline, and unit cohesion that are the essence of military capability.' The law even prohibits gays/lesbians in the armed forces from disclosing or discussing their sexuality on threat of discharge from the services. There was a certain irony that the first person to be wounded in the Iraq war was a gay marine.

The title is supposed to work on three levels. I saw it as one lover asking another, 'Would you take me home for Christmas and meet the family?' and then every gay person in the military asking, 'Will you take me into your hearts this Christmas, as I fight beside you?' and finally as the whole army and country saying, 'Get us outta this war by Christmas.'

As well as being a tribute to all the troops in battle, I wanted to highlight the hypocrisy of the DADT situation and lyrically I used a personalised, fictitious story to underline the sacrifices these people are making on our behalf only to be treated like freaks and outcasts.

I've received correspondence from one infantryman in Iraq who has said that *Naked And Finally Free* is the soundtrack for him and his team as they drive around there doing what they have to do. I don't know if he is gay or not but he says that the music has given them the spiritual sustenance to keep them going, with death peering constantly over their shoulder. To hear that is totally humbling, has so much more value than wealth or fame. They shower me with letters and gifts, but the real treasure is that they could get that from the music.

The whole world, including the US was behind going into Afghanistan after 9/11 and rooting out Al Qaeda and the Taliban, who alone had committed such atrocities, especially against women. But Bush dropped the ball. Allowing Afghanistan to fester into what it has become ten years later, and Iraq only a success in the eyes of the military-industrial complex, mainly Dick Cheney's Halliburton company, has proven a complete disaster. Bin Laden must have been laughing himself stupid having set in a motion a stream of events meant to hurt the US economically, only to see them do a better job of it themselves. At the moment Pakistan looks about to fall, along with their nukes. Iran is only stronger after Iraq and the US economy is looking like every empire that has fallen before it, never believing it could happen to them.

In Iraq, the motivation is not only the oil, but the water, the Tigris river that will prove so valuable, and having another nation in the US camp, as though the Cold War were still going on.

It has all stemmed from an out-of-control US Christian Fundamentalism, which reaches into the highest parts of US government, and nations around the world. It was at its zenith in the second Bush era as they were one and the same but even now it is very powerful in using its influence to restrict what Obama can do.

So the people of Iran, the women in particular, used to have this freedom, then had it taken away and that's just the most terrible thing. It upsets me hearing that today Iran has a serious heroin problem, because that will make the youth too lethargic to do anything about their situation. I guess it feels like their only escape. Afghanistan is the world's leading producer of heroin and borders Iran. Most of the heroin destined for the rest of the world goes through Iran. The whole thing is a mess.

The era of the Shah of Iran perfectly illustrates the principle by which America uses its power in a misguided way that has led to many of the problems currently faced by the world. Iran, and Saudi Arabia for that matter, unlike most other countries that are 'arm-twisted' into taking on debt, was modernised by giving its vast oil revenues to US mega-corporations to build dams, roads and power stations there. For most poor countries it is just a transference of funds from the US tax base to their corporate friends in America in exchange for keeping the current dictator in power. In effect the money never leaves the US. The deal with the Saudis was a promise to always keep that family in power. Elsewhere we have got into bed with despicable dictators so long as they played ball with America, and voted a certain way in the UN: Indonesia's Suharto, Idi Amin in Uganda and his replacement Yoweri Museveni, Jonas Savimbi in Angola, Somalia's Siad Barre, Brazil's General Costa e Silva, Papa Doc, Emperor Selassie, Noriega. The list of tyrants with heinous crimes against humanity who have been supported by America is endless. John Perkins' *Confessions of an Economic Hit Man* is a must-read book which lays out how it works way better than I can do justice for in these few lines.

There was a time when if we were in war, everybody would pull their weight, accept higher taxes and together we would win necessary wars, such as with Hitler. But now a set of ultra-wealthy Americans, Republicans mainly, want to pay less taxes, cut back on helping the poor, and borrow the money from the Chinese, the Saudis or even Iran, to pay for it. They should be embarrassed by the selfish greed, the unabashed gloating over having forced Obama's hand, by holding back things like the START treaty, and unemployment insurance from the poor who have had to shoulder the biggest burden during this economic downturn. The banks and Wall Street people, who were bailed out by the poor, are enjoying record profits despite their complicity in the current economic state of affairs. Their debts are public – in that we all have to pay for them – but their profits are privatised. They do this with ease, as though they feel entitled – as though they are the new chosen ones. They think they must govern the masses – who don't know what's good for them – to serve their needs.

During the Bush years, it all got way out of control. I even began rooting for the US military leaders as they tried to rein-in an out-of-control civilian leader. It's supposed to be the other way round! These may not be commercial things for me to be saying, but I am increasingly feeling the need to think about and express such things. Over the years there seems to have formed an increasingly calculated attempt to create the pretence of some sort of Disneyland – you see it reflected in TV reality shows, *American Idol* , *X Factor*, fairy tale lyrics and movies – to sort of drug us into not registering the reality of what is really happening in the world. We need to be taking a more active interest in the way our taxes are used around the world, what is being done in our name and finding out why 'the terrorists hate us'. I don't want to be complicit in the cover-up and if we behave like peasants in allowing this 'elite' to do whatever they want, then we are to blame.

With the world in such a parlous state, it was with great hope I watched Barack Obama gain his unstoppable momentum on the way to becoming US President. Boy does the world ever need a smart, black leader at the moment? What clinched it for me was his wife Michelle. My initial reaction to her was negative but then I saw her speak without notes. She speaks like Aretha sings, with that sparseness but then huge power. It was obvious that him and her together were one mighty force. Shortly after he announced his candidacy I was inspired to write 'Yes We Can'. I was taking a shower and the idea of that song just hit me.

I was flattered that my song was used – among others – during the campaign to get the crowd going before he came on. The momentum of that campaign just built and built and long before election day it was a done deal he was going to get in. When the result was confirmed a picture of me and the words 'Free's Andy Fraser says All Right Now' flashed up around Times Square and that image was circulated by PRNewswire.

So far Obama has been limited by his opponents in what he can do and I don't honestly know whether it will work out. I still give him a chance but if he gets sucked into that Washington warp I think I – and many others – would just give up on politics altogether. This guy is one of the most decent, energetic, inspiring figures to come along in living memory. But right now Washington is so screwed there are no guarantees.

Climate change is the biggest thing facing us all, threatening the very existence of humanity into the future. As I became ever-more aware of the issue, so I have incorporated it into my work. The song 'The Big One' is an attempt at bringing the message home.

I had just received a letter from the Tck Tck Tck campaign. In plain language it laid out the situation in a way that brought it home to me for the first time. It inspired me and I copy/pasted some of the phrases on that newsletter then went and took a shower. While it was washing over me the melody and rhythm came to me and I could already see the finished song. I went to the bass and started warbling some of the words I'd copy/pasted and in no time at all I had seven verses. I had to bring it down to two-and-a-half and voila: the song. It was on YouTube within two weeks of receiving that newsletter. The video company I work with is owned by a guy called Eric Donaldson and he's an activist on the subject and so was really fired up to get it out there in super-quick time.

ALL RIGHT NOW

Illustrating how long are the tentacles of the past, one day recently Andy received an e-mail from the wife of Nick Judd, his old keyboard player from the Andy Fraser Band. Attached to the message was a music file. Andy listened to it and what he heard blew him away. It was the moment when his focus shifted from his own music to that of someone else's for the first time since working with Frankie Miller.

Nick's wife Jane works at a theatre school for young actors and artists in London, the Bull Theatre. One of her pupils was this fifteen-year-old kid Tobias Earnshaw, Tobi for short, actually the son of the school's headmaster, David, who himself is an ex-session sax player. I could barely believe that what I was hearing was from this young kid. He was playing guitar like a mix of Hendrix, Clapton, Stevie Ray Vaughan and John Mayall and singing like some sort of cross between Michael Jackson, Sade, Robin Thicke and Michael McDonald, if you can imagine that. There was such a great sense of phrasing and rhythm. Besides, he was writing his own stuff. I immediately knew this kid had it; it was spectacular.

Up until hearing Tobi I was working on not just my own album, *On Assignment*, but also on my own music delivery system, Mctrax. It has a streaming and download capability that you can link to your computer, phone, XBOX, whatever. The CD is almost as dead as vinyl, streaming is where it's at and is much more green. *On Assignment* and a concert documentary of mine called *Alive* were going to be the first things released on this system. But the idea is not only to release my own stuff through it but to support and manage other artists. Tobi became our first signing.

After hearing his stuff I contacted Jane and found out more. He's from a unique family, just steeped in showbusiness. Aside from his dad having been in the music business for years and running the theatre school – Amy Winehouse attended there a few years ago – his mother Suzi runs a young actors' management firm from the same premises. Tobi would be attending the school until mid-2011. There had already been interest from the major labels but his family weren't sure if it was the right thing – and besides the labels seemed a little uncertain about taking him on while he was still attending school. I actually looked upon that as a great advantage as it potentially meant we could develop the whole project during that time.

It grew from there. We exchanged music files between LA and London and our first meeting was on Skype when I thought he handled himself extremely well for a fifteen-year-old talking to a fifty-seven-year-old. Very cool and mature.

I invited him and his father David across to LA and we hit it off immediately. They stayed for three weeks and we really got to know each other and laid down a lot of guitar and vocals in my studio here, the foundation of an album that we planned to release together in mid-2011. I provided bass and backing vocals and produced it. I get on great with David, he's very musically minded – he did the sax solos on quite a few pop hits – and easy to have a good laugh with. He has a good ear. Tobi couldn't have hoped for better parents and they encourage and support him 100 per cent.

It was incredible working with Tobi. When we started playing together the age difference just dissolved. He wasn't the least bit intimidated by me – in fact he pulled some very funny 'gotchas' on me. Easy to fall for because he's very low key. Like I'd be sitting there driving the car, wondering why my ass is roasting – and it's because he's been at the seat heaters when I wasn't watching, and sitting there looking totally innocent. Musically, I could see him evolving almost by the day and his ability is just phenomenal. He writes and sings from the heart, is not afraid to show vulnerability and has a decency, honesty and integrity about him that shines through in his music. He has the ability to cover both a pop audience and the rock concert arena crowd. I think he will be a huge star.

His youth, drive, freshness, and contemporary thinking have been a real inspiration to me. Playing bass alongside his guitar while we are working up the songs, the growth in his playing over those three weeks was staggering. He's constantly experimenting, discovering things. It's great to see a young, hungry mind looking to the future, seeing no limitations, and fully in a learning/discovery mode, as opposed to a tired, old re-tread one. It's really given me a stimulus for my own work.

Although he's very softly-spoken, one senses a quiet strength, a determination, intelligence and maturity and he trusts his instincts. He's unabashedly a romantic, as the songs to his girlfriend show, clearly able to feel free to express that, whereas most teenagers wouldn't say such things for their parents to hear, and with his looks he is gonna be a lady-killer. He has a strong sense of humour. He will play those video games on his iPad for hours, then I'll say, 'OK, let's do a vocal,' and, 'Boom' he's right in there. He has an amazing ability to focus. We did a video shoot, which started with some 'power clothes shopping' with Hannah who really has an eye, then we did a full day's shoot, with a two-hour drive back, and he still would be jotting down lyrics on his Blackberry on the way back. We were all knackered, but still his mind wasn't wasting a second.

I know I was similarly young when I started and back then it was do or die together. But with Tobi I do feel a sense of responsibility that is different from other musicians I have worked with; I feel that it's on me to make it right for him and it's a new experience for me. Most of the time it's just like talking to any other musician, we're on the same wavelength. When you're playing bass with the other guy on guitar you quickly get a sense of the other person – and we both just groove. In fact I mainly just lay back and listen in amazement at his ease, sense of freedom and adventure. But occasionally something will remind me he's only sixteen.

In the future I see myself helping other artists too, but staying personally involved, the alternative to the corporate approach. I'm still planning to do my own stuff but maybe have Tobi to add guitar etc. So although there's been a slight shift of focus, I'm not stopping anything, just adding. I wish there were thirty-six hours in the day though.

How many sixteen-year-olds could have slipped so apparently effortlessly into the fast lane of the music industry, have such confidence in their own ability? Well, there was another, forty-odd years ago. Pan back from Tobi and there, on bass, directing it all, taking it all in, the calm root at the centre of it all, is Andy. Still doing his stuff, despite everything the years have thrown at him. Totally relaxed in his skin now. All Right Now.

END

Ingram Content Group UK Ltd.
Milton Keynes UK
UKHW021528290323
419359UK00008B/991